SHOULD WE LET THE BOMB SPREAD?

SHOULD WE LET THE BOMB SPREAD?

EDITED BY

HENRY D. SOKOLSKI

NONPROLIFERATION POLICY EDUCATION CENTER

Cover design by Amanda Sokolski

CONTENTS

INTRODUCTION

Is Nuclear Proliferation Still a Problem?

Henry Sokolski

In 1966, Leonard Beaton, a journalist and strategic scholar, published a short book that asked must the bomb spread.[1] Mr. Beaton's query reflected the profound alarm with which proliferation was viewed shortly after the Cuban Missile Crisis. Today that alarm is all but absent: Now, not only is proliferation increasingly viewed as a given (more of a fact than a problem), but some security experts actually see advantages in nuclear weapons spreading or, at least, little harm.

Cultivation of this latter view took time—nearly a half century—and considerable scholarship. In 1981, Kenneth Waltz popularized French and American finite deterrence thinking of the late 1950s by asking whether or not nuclear weapons in more hands might be better. His answer was yes. As nuclear weapons spread, he argued, adversaries would view war as being self-defeating and peace would become more certain.[2]

---

1. Leonard Beaton, *Must the Bomb Spread?* (London: Penguin Books, 1966).

2. Cf. Kenneth Waltz, "The Spread of Nuclear Weapons: More May Be Better," *Adelphi Paper*, No. 171, (London: International Institute for Strategic Studies, 1981); Pierre-Marie Gallois, *Stratégie del'Age Nucléaire* (Paris: Francois-Xavier de Guibert, 1960); Commander P. H. Backus, "Finite Deterrence, Controlled Retaliation," *US Naval Institute Proceedings* 85, No. 3, (March, 1959): 23-29; and David Alan Rosenberg, "The Origins of Overkill: Nuclear Weapons and American Strategy 1945-1960," *International Security* 7, No. 4, (Spring 1983):

Although this view gained a certain following, some pushed back, emphasizing the real limits of nuclear safety and security. Drawing on official documents, Scott Sagan in the early 1990s detailed many nuclear accidents and near calls the U.S. military had with its nuclear arsenal. He and others also focused on the risks of illicit and unauthorized use and the chance that one side or another might misread the warning signals of a possible nuclear attack and respond when they should not.[3]

After the events of September 11, 2001, the question of whether terrorists might go nuclear—a worry studied in the early 1970s—regained urgency.[4] This concern, though, immediately raised yet another issue: Was nuclear deterrence, which the world's super-powers had relied upon so much during the Cold War, relevant any longer for dealing with nuclear-armed rogue states and terrorists?[5] Once joined with enthusiasm for going to zero nuclear weapons, this question gave rise to the notion that nuclear weapons were only marginally useful to deter the most likely forms of nuclear and non-nuclear aggression (thus, highlighting how dubious the possession or acquisition of nuclear weapons might be). More radical nuclear abolitionists went even further. For them, the bomb either didn't de-

3-71.

3. See Scott D. Sagan, *The Limits of Safety: Organizations, Accidents, and Nuclear Weapons* (Princeton: Princeton University Press, 1995); and Idem, "The Perils of Proliferation: Organization Theory, Deterrence Theory, and the Spread of Nuclear Weapons," *International Security*, Vol. 18, No. 4, (Spring 1994): 66-107.

4. Cf. Mason Willrich and Theodore B. Taylor, *Nuclear Theft: Risks and Safeguards: A Report to the Energy Policy Project of the Ford Foundation* (New York: Ballinger, 1974); Brian Jenkins, *Will Terrorists Go Nuclear?* (Santa Monica: RAND Corporation: P-5541, November 1975); Idem., *Will Terrorists Go Nuclear?* (Amherst: Prometheus Books, 2008); and Graham Allison, *Nuclear Terrorism: The Ultimate Preventable Catastrophe* (New York: Holt Paperbacks, 2005).

5. See e.g., William J. Perry, "Preparing for the Next Attack," *Foreign Affairs*, November/December 2001; and "Text of Bush's Speech at West Point," *The New York Times*, June 1, 2002, available at *www.nytimes.com/2002/06/01/international/02PTEX-WEB.html?pagewanted=all*.

ter or hardly deterred at all.[6] With this later perspective, it was but a small step to conclude that nuclear proliferation was neither good nor bad, but inconsequential.

But is it? Certainly, since 1966, the bomb has spread. Besides the United States, Russia, the United Kingdom, France, and China; Israel, India, Pakistan, and North Korea all acquired nuclear weapons. In addition, South Korea, Sweden, Taiwan, Iraq, Brazil, Argentina, Australia, and Iran all tried but did not get the bomb. So far, so good. But more proliferation in the Far and Middle East is possible (e.g., Iran, Saudi Arabia, Turkey, Algeria, Egypt, Taiwan, South Korea, and Japan).

Meanwhile, support for nuclear use is on the rise. Russia and Pakistan now favor the first use of nuclear weapons either to deter or to de-escalate future conventional conflicts. This has prompted India and China to review their nuclear use policies. What might happen if any of these states fired their weapons in anger and some military advantage was thereby secured? At least one respected military thinker argues that this would likely unleash a torrent of nuclear proliferation and far worse.[7]

For all of these reasons, nuclear deterrence no longer enjoys the almost religious support it once did. But perhaps that loss of faith is misplaced. After all, America's key allies—e.g., Japan and South Korea—still believe U.S. nuclear guarantees are critical to their survival. If they believe this and the United States is unwilling to provide Tokyo or Seoul with the nuclear assurance they desire, would it then not make sense for them to acquire nuclear forces of their own? This question is the basis of U.S. President-elect Donald Trump's ruminations about the inevitability and possible

---

6. See e.g., Ward Wilson, "The Myth of Nuclear Deterrence," *The Nonproliferation Review*, 15, No. 3, (November 2008): 421-439; and James E. Doyle, "Why Eliminate Nuclear Weapons?" *Adelphi Paper* 55, No.1, (February 1, 2013): 7-34.

7. Andrew W. Marshall, Foreword to *Underestimated: Our Not So Peaceful Nuclear Future*, by Henry Sokolski (Arlington: The Nonproliferation Policy Education Center, 2016), xi-xii.

value of Japan and South Korea going nuclear and Foreign Minister Boris Johnson's speculation that we would be better served if Iran acquired nuclear weapons.[8]

With more nuclear-armed states, and even one or two states more willing to use them, though, how likely is it that nuclear deterrence and no first-use will prevail? Is the sum of all fears—a nuclear apocalypse of the sort Mr. Beaton once wrote about—again in prospect? Getting the answers to these questions or, at least, raising them is this volume's purpose. In it, six experts offer a variety of perspectives sure to catalyze further debate.

In the book's first chapter, Harvey Sapolsky, the former director of the Massachusetts Institute of Technology's (MIT) Security Studies Program, makes a case that preventing nuclear proliferation, especially with nuclear security guarantees to our closest allies—Japan, South Korea and the North Atlantic Treaty Organization (NATO)— is unnecessary, provocative, and costly. Nuclear deterrence and forensics, he argues, will work and letting our allies go nuclear would be a safer, cheaper course than trying to prevent others from acquiring nuclear weapons and the U.S. basing forces overseas.

Seth Carus, who served in the Office of the Secretary of Defense and the Office of the Vice President, now is resident at the National Defense University's Center for the Study of Weapons of Mass Destruction as a distinguished fellow. He argues that such optimistic views are too academic. Those that serve in government, he notes, essentially ignore such arguments and with cause. Instead, he observes, senior policymakers worry about the destructiveness of

---

8. Maggie Haberman and David E. Sanger, "Transcript: Donald Trump Expounds on His Foreign Policy Views," *The New York Times*, March 26, 2016, available at *http://www.nytimes.com/2016/03/27/us/politics/donald-trump-transcript. html?_r=0*; Anderson Cooper, "Townhall in Milwaukee with Donald Trump-Transcript," *CNN,* March 29, 2016, available at *http://transcripts.cnn.com/TRAN-SCRIPTS/1603/29/acd.02.html*; and Boris Johnson, "Give Iran the bomb: it might make the regime more pliable," *The Telegraph,* October 12, 2006, available at *http://www.telegraph.co.uk/comment/personal-view/3633097/Give-Iran-the-bomb-it-might-make-the-regime-more-pliable.html*.

nuclear weapons and the fragility of nuclear deterrence between various states. They also are eager to maintain U.S. power against emerging nuclear states and to avoid the crisis instabilities further nuclear proliferation would prompt.

John Mueller, the author of Atomic Obsession, views these concerns as dangerous alarmism. Rather than arguing that nuclear proliferation is a positive development, Mueller makes the case that so far, nuclear proliferation has been far more benign than predicted and should be viewed as being largely inconsequential. In contrast, promoting nuclear nonproliferation, he argues, has produced war (e.g., Iraq), encouraged extortion (e.g., by North Korea), risked further wars (e.g., Iran), and deprived the world of the full benefits of civilian nuclear power.

This then brings us to former U.S. Nuclear Regulatory Commissioner Victor Gilinsky's chapter, "Should We Let It All Go?" Gilinsky concedes there is much to like about John Mueller's argument. He spotlights Mueller's questioning of the value of nuclear weapons threats or use, his critique of politicians and analysts who have been alarmist about nuclear terrorism, and his challenging of America's vacuous demands and threats regarding Iran's nuclear program. Gilinsky, however, insists that in arguing that proliferation hardly matters at all, that up to now its effects have been benign, and that efforts to restrain proliferation have done far more harm than good, Mueller goes too far. The bomb has had a significant impact on history. There certainly have been some close nuclear calls (e.g., the Cuban Missile Crisis). It also is the case that few, if any, of the bomb's possessors have been all that eager to give their weapons up. As for the harm nonproliferation has done, Gilinsky points out that such arguments mistakenly assume America's nonproliferation policies have had real teeth. It certainly is wrong, Gilinsky argues, to believe that nonproliferation was why we invaded Iraq. Gilinsky's conclusion: It would be unwise to relax whatever nuclear controls we still have and smarter still to strengthen them.

But is the prospect for nuclear use real? Matthew Kroenig and Rebecca Davis Gibbons of Georgetown University argue that the answer is yes. In their essay, the authors not only review the history of possible nuclear use during the Cold War, they lay out why and how Russia, China, North Korea, Israel, India, Pakistan, and the United States might nonetheless use these weapons first.

This, of course, begs the question as to what the consequences might be. Matthew Fuhrmann of Texas A&M University spells them out. They include igniting a catalytic war capable of dragging the nuclear superpowers in, creating massive destabilizing refugee crises, prompting international demands for regime change, encouraging the substitution of repressive rule for open forms of self-government, and the erosion of international norms against nuclear proliferation and use. None of these consequences are inevitable but likely enough to encourage all states to avoid first use if they can. The further spread of nuclear weapons might conceivably be beneficial, but the potential regret if their spread makes matters worse is easily large enough to recommend a less playful conclusion.

CHAPTER 1

Getting Past Nonproliferation

Harvey M. Sapolsky

The nuclear nonproliferation regime has lost its benefits, modest though they may have been, for the United States. In the post-Cold War era, the United States is burdened by friends who happily shun the possession of nuclear weapons along with most of the other expensive attributes of military self-defense, preferring instead our too freely offered nuclear security guarantees. We offer these guarantees, known as extended deterrence, to discourage them from acquiring nuclear weapons of their own. I fear, however, we have more to fear as a nation from the costs of extended deterrence—the costs for providing conventional defenses for friends, which is, in fact, the essence of our security guarantees—than from the need to deter additional nuclear-armed enemies, which is the potential result of the end of the nuclear nonproliferation regime.

The Nuclear Nonproliferation Treaty (NPT) when it was implemented in 1970 surely had important benefits for the Soviet Union and China because most of the states that might have acquired nuclear weapons during the Cold War—West Germany and Japan in particular, but Sweden, Australia, and others as well—would have targeted their weapons on the Soviet Union and China. The United Kingdom and France, fading powers that they were, probably liked the special status the NPT offered, and, if only for historical reasons, the fact that West Germany would not become a nuclear power. For the United States, the NPT deflected domestic attention away from the war in Vietnam with the hope of détente with the

8 *Should We Let the Bomb Spread*

Soviet Union, its necessary partner in the then promising quest to prevent the spread of nuclear weapons.[1]

The United States likely also wanted to avoid having West Germany, in particular, independently nuclear-armed if that meant needlessly provoking the Soviet Union. West Germany and Japan had by the mid-1960s recovered significantly from the Second World War and were seeking normal nation status. Germany was becoming an economic powerhouse, and Japan was not far behind. Nuclear-armed, they certainly would have been seen as more frightening to nations they had so recently occupied during the Second World War. The NPT provided the easy way to avoid a mid-Cold War crisis. There would be no West German or Japanese bomb.

There was also a post-Cold War NPT benefit for the United States.[2] The collapse of the Soviet Union cleared the way for Pax Americana, the brief period of American triumphalism in which the United States became the unelected and uncompensated global sheriff involved in suppressing, by force, if necessary, all sorts of international disputes, civil wars, and criminal behavior. The NPT was a facilitator for this volunteer work because only nations with nuclear weapons stood free from the sheriff's writ. Those without nuclear weapons were at risk of a visit from the law in the form of the American military. The several unhappy experiences of the boldly defined Global War on Terror has lately tempered the United States' interest in being the global sheriff and with it the special benefit to

1. Thomas Alan Schwartz, *Lyndon Johnson and Europe: In the Shadow of Vietnam* (Cambridge, MA: Harvard University Press, 2003), 206-222; John Dumbrell, "LBJ and the Cold War," in *A Companion to Lyndon B. Johnson* ed. Mitchell B. Lerner (Malden, MA: Blackwell Publishing, 2012) 431-435; and Francis J. Gavin, "Intelligence, Non-Proliferation, and the Shift in U.S. Policies in the 1960s" (paper presented at the conference "Intelligence and Prediction in an Unpredictable World," Center for International Security and Arms Control, Stanford University, Stanford, CA, June 2003).

2. Francis J. Gavin, "How Dangerous? History and Nuclear Alarmism," in *A Dangerous World? Threat Perception and National Security*, ed. Christopher A. Preble and John Mueller (Washington: CATO Institute, 2014), 20.

the United States of the NPT.[3] It is now the costs of nonproliferation that loom large, most specifically the need to provide a nuclear
shield plus conventional defenses for those who have foresworn
their own nuclear weapons. And because that shield is potentially
dangerous to offer and to trust, it is buttressed by forward deployed
conventional defenses that are quite robust to avoid the need to escalate to the use of nuclear weapons if the shield is tested.

Paying for Nonproliferation

The costs of the treaty did not seem great to the existing nuclear
powers at the time of its implementation. The NPT did require that
they pledge their intent to work toward their own disarmament
though with no stated measure of sincerity or progress. Nuclear
arms have in fact been reduced—thousands of American and Russian warheads have been taken out of service and dismantled—but
this was a result of the wind down of the Cold War and the resulting
desire to reap the benefits of reduced defense spending. The treaty
also explicitly protected the nuclear weapon states' commercial nuclear opportunities by assuring all nations access to nonmilitary nuclear technologies. It is through this doorway that nuclear materials
flow globally and, some fear, proliferators step through claiming
their peaceful desire for environmentally friendly nuclear energy
and the understandable hope of medical treatment and research.[4]

Beyond the usual Soviet menace, Warsaw Pact members needed
no special inducements to sign the NPT. The Soviet Union, after

---

3. Dov S. Zakheim, "Abandon Nation Building," *The National Interest* 131
(May/June 2014): 38-45.

4. According to the Leveretts, Iran is just interested in a civilian nuclear power
program in getting all those centrifuges on line. See Flynt Leverett and Hillary
Mann Leverett, "What's Really at Stake in the Impasse over Centrifuges-Hillary
Mann Leverett on the Iran Nuclear Talks," Going to Tehran, July 25, 2014, available from *goingtotehran.com/whats-really-at-stake-in-the-impasse-over-centri-
fuges-hillary-mann-leverett-on-the-iran-nuclear-talks*.

all, provided them with nuclear deterrence of a sort whether they wanted it or not. They had no option for acquiring nuclear weapons on their own. The Pact nations were the frontier buffer for the Soviet state, a tank's drive from the fearsome North Atlantic Treaty Organization (NATO) enemy, and were treated as such. In contrast, the United States' European NATO allies were fully aware that a big ocean lay between them and their protector. They sought constant reassurance that the United States would not abandon them in the face of nuclear threats. Acquiring nuclear weapons on their own was indeed an option for the allies. Right up to the NPT, various schemes were considered including a NATO nuclear force and the basing of dual-keyed U.S. tactical nuclear weapons around Europe to head this off. As an inducement for Europeans to accept the NPT, the United States—while retaining operational control over the weapons—allowed West Germany, Belgium, the Netherlands, Italy, and Turkey to modify certain aircraft to be capable of carrying U.S. tactical nuclear weapons based in their countries. Strangely, this practice continues today, though on a reduced scale.[5]

In fact, extended deterrence was not a major issue for the United States during the Cold War.[6] The United States believed that a Soviet-dominated Eurasia, like an Axis Power-dominated Eurasia—the threat of the Second World War—was an intolerable danger to its own viability and required challenge. U.S. forces were forward deployed in Europe because its allies, devastated by the Second World

---

5. On the tactical weapons in Europe issue see Barry Blechman and Russell Rumbaugh, "Bombs Away: The Case for Phasing Out U.S. Tactical Nukes in Europe," *Foreign Affairs* 93, no. 4 (July/August 2014): 163-174. The renewal of these weapons is now buttressed with claims that their modernization and continued presence will provide needed reassurance for Europeans made fearful by Russian ventures in the Ukraine, see Ralph Vartabedian and W.J. Hennigan, "US nuclear arsenal in Europe is likely to stay," *Stars and Stripes*, September 21, 2014, available from *www.stripes.com/news/europe/us-nuclear-arsenal-in-europe-is-likely-to-stay-1.304222.*

6. Extended deterrence hardly merited discussion in Lawrence Freedman's masterful study of nuclear strategy, *The Evolution of Nuclear Strategy, 2nd Edition* (New York: St. Martin's Press, 1989), 290, 424.

War, were unable to provide an effective barrier to potential Soviet expansion into Western Europe. The United States saw the Communist side as having a numerical, conventional warfare advantage and wanted any confrontation to be sobered by the danger of nuclear escalation. Our forces were there as a tripwire to guarantee a challenge at the boundary of NATO or the borders of our Asian allies would, by threatening U.S. forces directly, involve great risk to the United States and possible counter nuclear strikes, or even a preemptive strike by the United States.

The Korean War seemed to American leaders like both the opening round of an all-out war with the Soviet Union and a diversion to take the focus off the main front in Europe. The Korean contest, though soon stalemated, was replaced by another in Vietnam that eventually also involved the United States. Asia during the Cold War featured the opposite of Europe—no direct confrontations of nuclear powers, weak alliance structures, and very intense land wars. But like the case in Europe, the United States freely offered up extended nuclear deterrence guarantees for all who wanted them among its major friends in Asia.[7]

Much has changed since the enactment of the NPT. The United States' allies in Europe and Asia are now among the richest nations in the world. Japan has the world's third-largest economy while the now united Germany has the fourth and is the leading economy in the European Union. The main threats to our security are attacks on American soil by non-state entities, none of which possess nuclear weapons. The Soviet Union has collapsed into a smaller, less important, less powerful Russia. China is now a major American trading partner and growing rapidly, but is mainly focused on the domestic stability impacts of that growth and not on international expansion. The wars in Iraq and Afghanistan confirm the difficulty in America acting as the sheriff in distant lands where effective, representative, non-corrupt local governments are unknown and

---

7. New Zealand seemingly renounced its extended deterrence, though never explicitly.

seemingly impossible to create.[8] The need for forward deployment of U.S. forces has greatly diminished.

Overextended

Absurdly, extended deterrence remains a cornerstone of U.S. foreign policy. The United States still promises to exchange Washington for Berlin and San Francisco for Tokyo. And even more absurdly, the nuclear guarantee now extends to former Warsaw Pact states and former Soviet republics that have become NATO members, making their borders the West's frontier. In Asia, North Korea, having withdrawn from the NPT,[9] has acquired nuclear weapons, and China, now more militarily powerful and politically assertive, is pressing claims for islands administered by other nations including our friends.[10] It is now Boston for Riga and Seattle for Seoul that is at risk. The cries for reassurance on the part of allies are more persistent given how implausible the promise is now to provide nuclear deterrence for allies.

In order to never have to contemplate such a deal, the United States provides its allies with conventional defenses. We guard Eastern Europe from a Russia still fuming about its lost empire and East Asia from the growing power of China. Our allies are fully capable of affording their own defenses, but provide neither sufficient conventional defenses nor their own nuclear shield. Worse, our allies tempt our fate by being cavalier about their relations with their status-sensitive, nuclear-armed neighbors. The European Union plays footsie with Ukraine, once Russia's breadbasket and home still to many

---

8. The futility is evident in James A. Russell, *Innovation, Transformation and War: Counter-insurgency Operations in Anbar and Ninewa Provinces, Iraq, 2005-2006* (Stanford, CA: Stanford University Press, 2011).

9. A. Wes Mitchell and Jan Havranek, "Atlanticism in Retreat" *The American Interest* 9, no. 2 (November/December 2013): 41-57, available from *http://www.the-american-interest.com/2013/10/10/atlanticism-in-retreat/*.

10. "Banyan: Force Majeure," *The Economist*, May 24, 2014, 38.

Russians while Japan and others have their coast guards sail dangerously close to Chinese vessels in jockeying over rocky outcrops.

Extended deterrence is no longer nuclear deterrence at a distance, but rather a conventional defense of our allies' borders. We do not see our forward deployed forces as a tripwire for nuclear escalation as they were viewed during the Cold War. Instead, they are intended to have the capability of winning the conventional fight so as to either deter it from occurring or keep it from escalating to the nuclear level. The means for gaining conventional warfare dominance has been the precision revolution, which is the development of systems that can precisely detect, target, and destroy opposing forces—in great numbers if necessary—with little or no collateral damage, most particularly no civilian casualties.[11] Nuclear weapons were essentially compensation for the inability of conventional bombing, even conducted on a massive scale, to destroy enemy capabilities because of its inaccuracies. Close was good enough with nuclear weapons. Now precision weapons are in essence the way to avoid the massive and indiscriminate destruction of nuclear weapons. They represent warfare coming full circle. First small bombs, then bigger and bigger bombs until their destructive capability is so enormous the target cannot be missed, and now back to small bombs, but ones so precise that the target is certain to be destroyed.

But weapons technology diffuses, nuclear or conventional. The sensors, guidance, networks, and missile systems that lie at the heart of the precision weapons revolution are spreading to potential opponents across the globe.[12] The cost of protecting towns bordering

---

11. For a history of precision see Paul E. Gillespie, *Weapons of Choice: The Development of Precision Guided Munitions* (Tuscaloosa, AL: University of Alabama Press, 2006).

12. Lynn E. Davis, Michael J. McNerney, James Chow, Thomas Hamilton, Sarah Harting, and Daniel Byman, "Armed and Dangerous? UAVs and US Security," (RAND Corporation RR 449, 2014), available from *rand.org/content/dam/rand/pubs/research_reports/RR400/RR449/RAND_RR449.pdf*; and Lt. Gen. David A. Deptula, USAF (Ret), "A New Era for Command and Control of Aerospace Operations," *Air & Space Power Journal* (July-August, 2014): 5-15, available from

Russia or islands near China is extraordinarily high and is certain to increase as their militaries modernize, acquiring more and more precision weapons. Trying to be the dominant conventional military at the border of big power opponents, but thousands of miles from our own shores is a formula for creating a huge military and ultimate bankruptcy. Our best policy, as it was in the world wars, is to put great distance between enemy forces and our own forces until enemy forces are heavily eroded, preferably through contact with our allies or other opponents. Such a policy today would encourage allies to both stiffen their conventional forces and acquire nuclear weapons. One comes with the other.

The so-called pivot to Asia is to provide reassurance to our Asia allies who worry about our ability to meet the challenge of a rising China.[13] They fear that we will abandon them as we are pushed aside in the Western Pacific by the increasing might of an ever richer China, one that has a long memory about its supposed humiliations at the hand of colonizers and empire builders, including Japan and the United States. They wonder whether or not we will fulfill pledges to save them from Chinese intimidation, including increased Chinese efforts to assert claims over waters known to be rich in fishing, and likely oil as well. All of this is taking place within the first island chain, the half ring of island nations that border China on its coastal frontier and that could help block its access to the open seas and thus the global resources needed for its continuing economic growth.[14]

The Asian pivot has so far brought with it only modest troop deployments and the repositioning of minor air and naval assets. Marines

---

http://www.au.af.mil/au/afri/aspj/digital/pdf/articles/2014-Jul-Aug/SLP-Deptula. pdf.

13. "Jittery Neighbors: Asian fears of China's rise," *The Economist*, July 19, 2014, 10, available from *www.economist.com/news/asia/21607869-worries-about-chinas-ascent-jittery-neighbours.*

14. James R. Holmes, "Defend the First Island Chain," *U.S. Naval Institute Proceedings* 140, No. 4 (April 2014): 32-37; Milan Vego, "Chinese Shipping Could Be Risky Business," *U.S. Naval Institute Proceedings* (April 2014): 38-43.

will be rotating through a training facility in Australia. American forces will have increased access to bases in the Philippines. Additional forces are being assigned to Guam. But the real challenge lies in operating within the first island chain, which is subject to China's ever increasing anti-access/area-denial capabilities—accurate cruise and tactical ballistic missiles, sophisticated mines, integrated air defense systems—that greatly threaten any serious attempts to protect allies from Chinese moves to assert territorial claims.[15]

Meeting the Chinese anti-access/area-denial challenge has become an obsession with elements of the American military, particularly the Air Force and the Navy, which are eager for new missions to champion after their relative fade post-9/11 when we fought less technologically sophisticated enemies. It is possible to imagine the combination of advanced intelligence, surveillance and reconnaissance capabilities, long-range conventional strike weapons, stealthy aircraft, submarines, anti-radiation missiles, agile missile defenses, and robust command and control systems that U.S. forces could mount that would permit survivable military operations close to the Chinese shore.[16] Doctrine for such capabilities is being devised under the rubric "air-sea battle" as are alternatives such as blockades and other submarine centric efforts.[17] Supportive weapons system developments are underway. No estimate has been released, but the cost of meeting the Chinese anti-access/area-denial challenge will

---

15. Lyle Goldstein and Shannon Knight, "Wired for Sound in the 'Near Sea,'" *U.S. Naval Institute Proceedings* (April 2014): 56-61; Andrew S. Erickson and Michael S. Chace, "China Goes Ballistic," *The National Interest* No. 131 (May/ June 2014): 58-64; and Jacqueline Newmyer Deal, "Red Alert," *The National Interest* (May/June 2014): 85-96.

16. Harry Foster, "The Joint Stealth Task Force: An Operational Concept for Air-Sea Battle," *Joint Forces Quarterly* 72 (1st Quarter 2014): 47-53.

17. Commander David Forman, USN, "The First Rule of Air-Sea Battle," *U.S. Naval Institute Proceedings* (April, 2014): 26-31; and Colonel Robert C. Boyles, "Air-Sea Battle Disclaimers and "Kill-Chains" *U.S. Naval Institute Proceedings* 140, No. 1 (January 2014): 46-51.

surely be hundreds of billions of dollars.[18]

Russia's grab of Crimea highlights a related challenge, defending Eastern Europe.[19] Of course, Russia is not the Soviet Union in terms of its inherent military power. Its population is smaller, its industrial focus less martial, and its military equipment less expeditionary, modern, and ready. Nevertheless, at its frontier, Russia is a formidable force, fully capable of defeating any opposition from its neighbors. Russian air defenses are cutting edge, and Russia possesses significant armor and special operations forces. Nuclear-armed and seeking to reclaim regional dominance, Russia is quite intimidating close up and happy to remind its neighbors that it is not to be trifled with by them.[20] We too must be careful about Russia if only because we need Russian assistance in many parts of the globe.[21]

Extended deterrence makes these military problems—the containment of potentially expansionary nations—not the burden of allies in their regions, but America's.[22] Free riding allies, wealthy though

---

18. The Marines are trying hard to get their share. See Colin Clark, "Marines Won't Take the Beaches Head-On anymore; Find the Gaps," *Breaking Defense*, June 26, 2014, available from *breakingdefense.com/2014/06/marines-wont-take-the-beaches-head-on-any-more-find-the-gaps/*.

19. Secretary General Anders Rasmussen and General Philip Breedlove, "A NATO for a Dangerous World" *Wall Street Journal*, August 18, 2014, available from *www.wsj.com/articles/anders-fogh-rasmussen-and-philip-m-breedlove-a-nato-for-a-dangerous-world-1408317653*.

20. Alexei Anishchuk, "Don't mess with nuclear Russia, Putin says," *Reuters*, August 29, 2014, available from *news.yahoo.com/putin-says-russia-ready-respond-aggression-123956691.html*; and Tony Osborne, "Facing Threats: Ukrainian crisis has prompted NATO to beef up defenses, but at what cost?" *Aviation Week & Space Technology* 176, No. 32 (September 15, 2014): 31.

21. Dimitri K. Simes, "Reawakening an Empire," *The National Interest* No. 132 (July/August 2014): 5-15.

22. See for example Chris Jennewein, "Top Admiral: Resource Competition, China's Rise Threaten Pacific," *Times of San Diego*, August 19, 2014, available from *timesofsandiego.com/military/2014/08/19/top-admiral-resource-competition-*

they may be, make little effort to protect themselves. Their defense budgets and militaries continue to decline. NATO's two percent budgetary goal, the percentage of gross domestic product to be devoted to defense, goes unmet.[23] Asian air and naval forces are slow to modernize. Their contributions to outset the costs of stationing U.S. forces forward nowhere near cover the true expenses--the training, equipping, and rotating of combat ready units. Worse, they tempt our fate by pushing at the edge. The European Union entices Ukraine to pull away from Russian influence while the ships of our Asian allies maneuver against Chinese ships near disputed islands. The question always is: What will we do to help them? The obligations are hardly ever reciprocal to any extent.

It is not just America's military that is at risk, but the American economy also. Acquired through the underfunding of past wars and the inefficiencies of a patchwork social safety net, the national debt has reached the 18 trillion dollar mark. It is certain to increase due to rising health care costs and the retirement of the generation that was born after the Second World War. Interest on the debt is projected soon to exceed our current inflated defense expenditures.[24] Because we invest so heavily in providing what is essentially free security to others, we lack the fine roads, the high-speed trains, and shiny airports of our European and Asian allies. Protecting the borders of these allies from the threat of intrusion by their militarily-capable neighbors, as extended deterrence policy requires us to do, is a financial burden that prevents those investments and a trimming of the national debt. Neglected infrastructure and a mounting

---

chinas-rise-threaten-pacific.

23. For NATO data see Naftali Bendavid, "Ukraine Simmers as Putin Digs In," *Wall Street Journal*, August 30/31, 2014, 1.

24. For number by 2020, see Douglas W. Elmendorf, Director, Congressional Budget Office, "Shifting Priorities in the Federal Budget," (presentation at Cornell University, September 11, 2014); note also, Wendy Edelberg, "CBO's Projection of Federal Interest Payments," *CBO Blog*, September 3, 2014, available from *www.cbo.gov/publication/45684.*

debt are significant threats to America's future prosperity.[25]

More Wars to Fight and Lies to Tell

The NPT has stopped neither wars nor, and more to its intended purpose, the spread of nuclear weapons. There are now nine nuclear powers instead of five as India, Israel, Pakistan, and North Korea have joined the club, though not formally. Nations fearing for their survival against powerful enemies think about acquiring nuclear weapons. With the NPT, their efforts have to be clandestine and de-termined, but for relatively rich and technologically sophisticated nations, it is a path that can be taken. India faces a nuclear-armed China allied with its rival Pakistan. Israel is surrounded by hostile Muslim nations increasingly swayed by jihadist ideology. Pakistan has the bigger, more powerful India to worry about. And North Ko-rea fears the United States.

Nuclear-armed nations are often at war, but not with each other. Nu-clear weapons sober regional tensions by giving great caution to ag-gressive actions. The dangers of escalation restrain the inclination to use even low levels of military force in disputes with nuclear-armed opponents. War is full of surprises, which makes it too dangerous for nuclear powers to fight one another. One miscalculation about likely opponent reactions could be one too many in any encounter.

Ironically, nuclear nonproliferation efforts can be both confron-tational and violent. Although not under the NPT banner, Israel bombed nuclear reactor sites in Iraq in 1981 and Syria in 2007 to prevent the acquisition of nuclear weapons by hostile nations. The United States invaded Iraq in 2003 claiming the enforcement of United Nations resolutions banning Iraqi possession of weapons of mass destruction. And today both Iran and North Korea labor under severe trade sanctions because of their development, and in

---

25. Stephen D. King, *When The Money Runs Out: The End of Western Influence* (New Haven, CT: Yale University Press, 2013).

North Korea's case acquisition, of nuclear weapons. Iran lives on the brink of war because Israel and the United States have said that neither will tolerate Iran becoming a nuclear weapons power.[26] If negotiations and sanctions fail to persuade Iran to limit its ambitions and accept intrusive inspections, attacks on Iran seem likely, and as Iran has pledged retaliation, an expanded war as well.[27]

The hard treatment is only for some. Israel, India, and Pakistan never signed the NPT. Because Israel's nuclear weapon status is unacknowledged, it is not subject to much discussion or any penalty. India and Pakistan did incur the wrath of the United States in the form of some unwelcomed sanctions and undelivered aid, but these penalties were lifted when their cooperation was needed in other matters. North Korea is an NPT signatory who renounced the treaty, but the animosity against it predates any North Korean interest in nuclear weapons.

The NPT creates two kinds of sovereignty: that possessed by states permitted to have nuclear weapons, the original five, and that possessed by all others, which are not permitted weapons. The embarrassing arrogance of it all is compensated by the treaty promise of the permitted nuclear powers to work toward nuclear disarmament. In an era of increased interest in equality, the pledge seems inadequate at best. How can there be nearly 200 sovereign nations and only five virtuous enough to be allowed to have the bomb? Thus, there is a growing interest in the so-called zero option, the claim expressed by various heads of state, including U.S. President Barack Obama, that the goal for the permitted nuclear powers is the elimination of all nuclear weapons.[28] Given that the knowledge

---

26. Matthew Kroeing, *A Time To Attack* (New York: Palgrave MacMillian, 2014).

27. Stopping the Iranian program is quite difficult. See Norman Friedman, "Learning to Love the (Iranian) Bomb," *U.S. Naval Institute Proceedings* (January 2014): 90-91.

28. But see John Mueller, "Think Again: Nuclear Weapons," *Foreign Policy*, December 19, 2009, available from *foreignpolicy.com/2009/12/18/think-again-*

needed to build nuclear weapons cannot be destroyed, and given the trust needed in the owner of the last weapon to be destroyed when all others have none, it is a goal likely never to be met and seems disingenuous in its offering. Anyone concerned about the likelihood of zero happening should be reassured to learn that all the weapon-possessing nations are in the process of upgrading their weapons and/or the platforms needed for the delivery of their weapons.[29] And one may wonder how Israel or North Korea will be persuaded to take the zero pledge.

Pro-Proliferation

With the treaty abandoned, not many nations will seek to acquire nuclear weapons. Most do not live in a tough neighborhood, have the technological base needed to carry out the task, wish to devote the resources to the cause, or welcome the responsibility of protecting them from accident, theft, and/or preemptive attack from worried neighbors. Ukraine may well regret giving up the Soviet weapons based on its territory to Russia, but the invasion risk and dollar cost of moving to acquire them afresh may be too much. Some in Libya probably regret giving up their program, as having retained it the Qaddafis would still be in power. The Libya of today is in no condition to revive it.

The lesson is that if you face a serious threat from a nuclear power on your own and have sufficient resources, you best go nuclear

---

nuclear-weapons/.

29. The bill is not small. The United States plans to spend $263.8 billion over through 2024 and Congress' watchdog, the Government Accountability Office thinks that number is an under estimate. Government Accountability Office, "Nuclear Weapons: Ten-Year Budget Estimates for Modernization Omit Key Efforts, and Assumptions and Limitations Are Not Fully Transparent" GAO-14-373, June 2014; and William J. Broad and David E. Sanger, "U.S. Ramping Up Major Renewal in Nuclear Arms," *New York Times,* September 22, 2014, 1.

quickly and quietly.[30] Canada likely would not because it receives
free extended deterrence in perpetuity by virtue of sharing a con-
tinent with the United States. Without the United States providing
the nuclear umbrella, however, Germany and Japan likely will go
nuclear. Their now largely self-imposed and budgetary convenient
exemption from any serious military obligations, including their
own defense, will surely evaporate without extended deterrence.
South Korea and Australia would also likely acquire nuclear weapons. South Korea has twice the population of the North and 25
times its wealth, but still claims it is not ready to manage its own
defense against the nuclear-armed but impoverished North. It pre-
fers the United States carry that burden. And Australia, living well
in a region of populous and expanding nations, will recognize how
far it actually is from the United States.

The fear, of course, is that without the NPT barrier, not just friendly
nations in Europe or Asia but also hostile, unstable, and/or terror-
ist-supporting regimes in the Middle East will go nuclear. A nuclear
weapon in their hands is more frightening than a nuclear weapon in
Russian and Chinese hands. How long will a nuclear-armed Saudi
Arabia survive as a kingdom? Wouldn't Iran give some to Hezbollah or Qatar and a couple to Hamas?

Deterrence and forensics work.[31] Nations that threaten the United
States will discover that they face a most formidable and tenacious
opponent. Post-NPT nuclear weapons will remain difficult to obtain, costly to protect, and very, very risky to gift, lend, or trade.
The extreme caution that applies to attacks on nuclear powers applies also to those who would hand nuclear weapons to their terrorist enemies as the links are sure to be revealed. Often the terrorists
are as much a threat to others as they are to the United States. The

30. Norman Friedman, "Keeping Putin in Check," *U.S. Naval Institute Proceed-ings* 140, No. 5 (May, 2014): 162-163.

31. The clearest on this is, as always, John Mueller. See his "Nuclear Alarm-ism: Proliferation and Terrorism," in *A Dangerous World? Threat Perception and U.S. National Security*, 25-39.

weapon that they steal from you may be used against you, so there is strong incentive to protect nuclear weapons from theft and against handing them to others.

Obstacles to Relinquishing the Burden

The biggest obstacle to getting beyond the NPT is the fear of terrorists using a stolen or otherwise nefariously obtained a nuclear weapon to blackmail or destroy civilization. Many a blockbuster novel, movie, and television program has this theme as its plot.[32] We have learned to live with Russians and Chinese, even those who are threatening, but not terrorists. Terrorists, we believe, have no bounds. We all are taught the destructive power of nuclear weapons. Just think what terrorists will do with them. There is an industry that stokes these fears, aided by reports of dropped or inadequately guarded weapons. If there were 15 or 20 nuclear-armed nations instead of 5 or 10, the opportunities for disaster would surely increase.

Given that the United States has the most extensive experience with nuclear weapon accidents and safeguards, we should widely share that knowledge.[33] Every new nuclear power upon the revelation of its new status should be offered a package of our hard-won ideas for safely maintaining, handling, and guarding nuclear weapons and any relevant training that it might require. A somewhat similar initiative helped protect Russian nuclear weapons in the period of semi-chaos that occurred after the collapse of the Soviet Union. Not all new nuclear powers would trust the friendly act, but all would recognize the importance others place on their custodial skills.

---

32. A recent favorite is Michael Weiss, *The Bomb on the Rock: A Tale of Two Sons* (self-published, 2013).

33. Gregory D. Koblentz, "Command and Combust: America's Secret History of Atomic Accidents," review of *Command and Control: Nuclear Weapons, the Damascus Accident, and the Illusion of Safety* by Eric Schlosser, *Foreign Affairs* 93, No. 1 (January/February, 2014): 167-172.

The American military is another obstacle to giving up the NPT. The American military adheres to a doctrine of forward deployment that is largely supported by the conventional warfare requirements of an extended deterrence foreign policy. Its command structure is based on joint regionally-focused commands that manage deployed forces and that take as their mission the tempering of regional conflicts via partnerships and direct action to avoid the risks of escalation. Much of its force levels are justified on the basis of regional conventional deterrence. Without other nations to protect at their boundaries, the United States would have a much smaller military.

The NPT has a civilian domestic lobby as well--the network of anti-nuclear weapons foundations, public interest groups, university programs, and proliferation monitoring agencies. The normal political divisions do not apply to nonproliferation advocates. They are on the left, right, and center. They are heard inside government and out. They are establishmentarian and radical. And they have the public forum to themselves. There is no counter lobby that advocates the spread of nuclear weapons. There are no marches in the United States for the proliferation of nuclear weapons.[34]

Although all the components of the nonproliferation lobby could not possibly agree on this formulation of their advocacy, nonproliferation is an advocacy for American hegemony in the Western world defined to include our Asian allies. The United States provides extended deterrence for all. It is the grand protector. Britain and France are extras, at best an afterthought. Because the United States takes the nuclear risk, it assumes to be the manager of global security, guarding the borders of all. The U.S. Navy tells us that it is the global force for good. The U.S. Air Forces boasts that it has global reach. And the U.S. Army is stationed in Europe, the Middle

---

34. But there have been some voices of reason. Note, Kenneth N. Waltz, "Why Iran Should Get the Bomb: Nuclear Balancing Would Mean Stability," *Foreign Affairs* 91, No. 4 (July/August, 2012): 2-5.

East, Japan, and Korea, about as global as an army can get.[35]

Learning to Let Others Love the Bomb

The NPT was made for the Cold War world in which there were two clearly defined sides and a possibility that every conflict could potentially lead to a nuclear exchange between them. It was right then to seek to limit the number of nuclear weapons states to avoid alliance complications. Some conflicts, however, existed independently of the Cold War. It is not that they were unaffected by the Cold War or did not have an effect of their own on it, but rather that they would have existed whether there was a Cold War or not. The Arab-Israeli conflict is one. The tension between India and Pakistan is another. It is not surprising that participants in these conflicts refused to sign the NPT and were the first to defy the intent of the treaty. When your survival is at stake, nuclear weapons have a special appeal.[36]

North Korea broke with the nonproliferation regime after the Cold War was over when its main protectors, China and Russia, no longer cared much about its fate. Also, its main antagonist, the United States, was at the time very much distracted by the two wars in which it was fighting elsewhere in the world. North Korea's motives for seeking nuclear weapons may have been mixed, but the announcement that it developed such a weapon no doubt gave it a lot of attention, some protection, and a bit of self-respect.

Since the end of the Cold War neither Russia, as the successor state to the Soviet Union, nor the United States believes that it is in mor-

---

35. For a very useful discussion of the role of the military and others in hyping our threats see Benjamin H. Friedman, "Alarums and Excursions: Explaining Threat Inflation in U.S. Foreign Policy,' in *A Dangerous World? Threat Perception and U.S. National Security*, 281-304.

36. For an analysis of the motives for acquiring and strategies for use of nuclear weapons in crises see Vipin Narang, *Nuclear Strategy in the Modern Era: Regional Powers and International Conflict* (Princeton, NJ: Princeton University Press, 2014).

tal danger from an unexpected strike from the other. Their nuclear forces stand on constant alert, and there is a concern by both to maintain a survivable second-strike capability, but their respective societal lives no longer hang solely on a nuclear thread. There are many disputes between them, but none comes close to raising nuclear alarms. As the strains on alert forces indicate, service in nuclear forces for the major powers is a backwater of boredom and career hibernation.

In contrast, the United States' Cold War friends have a number of contentious issues with Russia and China. None of these issues yet rise to the level of mortal danger, but the relations of American allies with both countries are definitely more frayed and volatile than those of the United States. American forces' presence near China or in Eastern Europe is for the reassurance of allies and not for the United States' own security. Similarly, South Korea and Japan want the United States to maintain its bases in their countries to protect them from their often hostile and always unpredictable North Korean neighbor. It is the North Korean bomb that worries them.[37]

No other nuclear power offers allies extended deterrence—not Russia, not France, not the United Kingdom, not Israel, and not India. The Chinese bomb protects China alone. Similarly, the Pakistani and the North Korean bombs guard only one country, their own. Nuclear deterrence, at its core, is a self-help program and never a charitable one.[38]

America's offer of extended deterrence is thus a very strange policy, sustainable only by a willingness to be involved deeply in the

37. Gerard Baker and Alastair Gale, "South Korean President Warns on Nuclear Domino Effect," *Wall Street Journal*, May 29, 2014, available from *www.wsj. com/articles/south-korea-president-park-geun-hye-warns-on-nuclear-domino-effect-1401377403.*

38. Richard K. Betts, "Universal Deterrence or Conceptual Collapse? Liberal Pessimism and Utopian Realism," in *The Coming Crisis: Nuclear Proliferation, U.S. Interests, and World Order,* ed. Victor A Utgoff (Cambridge, MA: MIT Press, 2000), 65.

security of distant nations, many of which have no obligation or capacity to reciprocate in any meaningful way.[39] No wonder American allies constantly seek reassurance of our interest in their defense.[40] It is to them surely an unbelievable policy both because of the risks it imposes on us and because of the huge subsidy it provides them in the form of the forward deployment of well-trained and equipped U.S. conventional forces.

It is also an unaffordable and outdated policy. Without the menace of the Soviet Union, the United States is militarily secure. Our Cold War allies are rich and can well afford their own defenses. We have no need to station significant forces in Europe or Asia. Instead, we have problems at home to tend to including mounting deficits, crumbling infrastructure, and too many young people who lack the skills to compete effectively with their global peers. These problems will likely be difficult to manage, but they require the resources that are now devoted to providing the frontier defenses of friends who prefer not to have to build and maintain their own nuclear weapons or even dress up in uniforms.

The bad habits of our allies are largely of our own making, but are buttressed by the nuclear nonproliferation regime.[41] The American military leans far forward quite willingly on the claim that local conflicts must be managed in order to prevent their potential escalation. The NPT makes our friends permanently vulnerable to nuclear co-

---

39. Thomas M. Nichols, *No Use: Nuclear Weapons and US National Security* (Philadelphia: University of Pennsylvania Press, 2013).

40. Doug Bandow, "Is Poland's Alliance with America 'Worthless?'" The National Interest, June 25, 2014, available from *nationalinterest.org/feature/poland%E2%80%99s-alliance-america-worthless-10748*.

41. Senior American officials past and present continue to claim to worry about whether America's allies will maintain their confidence in our commitment to their security. See the discussion of the recent National Defense Panel, the reviewing body of the Quadrennial Defense Report in, Evan Moore, "Why America Still Needs Nukes," *Real Clear Defense*, August 12, 2014, available from *realcleardefense.com/articles/2014/08/12/why_america_still_needs_nukes_107359.html*.

ercion and subtly shifts the burdens of their security too much onto the United States. It is the ultimate exemption from adult responsibility. Instead of trying to enforce the treaty the United States ought to be trying to get rid of it. Nuclear nonproliferation deceives no one but the American taxpayer.

CHAPTER 2

Why U.S. Policymakers Who Love the Bomb Don't Think "More is Better"[1]

W. Seth Carus

Disconnects between the academic and the policy worlds are not unusual. Nevertheless, it still is striking when an academic debate, supposedly about a topic of vital national security concern, rages for decades but is totally ignored by those responsible for policy-making in that arena. This is certainly true for the argument offered by some academics that nuclear proliferation contributes to the stability of the international system, arguing that "more is better." Yet, it would be difficult, perhaps impossible, to find any Washington policymaker accepting such a position. Indeed, during the past 50 years there has been a widespread consensus amongst U.S. policymakers, across the political and ideological spectrum, that "more is NOT better" and that nonproliferation efforts are an essential element of U.S. national security policy.

---

1. The views expressed in this article are those of the author and not necessarily those of the National Defense University or the Department of Defense. The author would like to thank his NDU colleagues, Dr. Thomas Blau, Dr. Susan Koch, and Dr. Mark Mattox, as well as the participants in the May 21, 2012 Nonproliferation Policy Education Center workshop on "Reassessing the Assumptions Driving Our Current Nuclear Nonproliferation Policies," for comments on an earlier draft of this chapter. In addition, Read Hanmer, Greg Koblentz, Clark Murdoch, Keith Payne, and Greg Schulte all offered constructive criticisms, although not all of their useful and insightful comments made it into the final version of the chapter. The author takes full responsibility for any remaining errors.

The pages that follow will start by first examining the views of the academics who espouse the "more is better" argument, followed by a review of some of the perspectives that explain why almost all U.S. national security policymakers have ignored it. Who are the policymakers in question? They include executive branch officials, starting with the last 12 presidents and continuing with their immediate advisors—national security advisors, secretaries of defense and state, and other senior officials (deputy secretaries, undersecretaries, and assistant secretaries of various departments), as well as many members of Congress. This discussion is focused exclusively on Washington and the men and women responsible for creating and executing U.S. national security policies. It does not address the potentially different perspectives of officials in other countries, who may operate using different rules and perceive the world in different ways.

Proliferation Optimists and Pessimists

In academic circles, nuclear proliferation "optimists" and "pessimists" argue over the dangers posed by the risks of the further spread of nuclear weapons. The proliferation optimists, represented articulately and starkly by Kenneth Waltz, argue that nuclear arsenals reduce the chances of armed conflict, and that the benefit from this reduction in conventional warfare means that "more is better" when it comes to nuclear proliferation.[2] Waltz's influence in this arena resulted in part from his towering status as a scholar of inter-

---

2. Waltz presented his views in Kenneth N. Waltz, "The Spread of Nuclear Weapons: More May Be Better," *Adelphi Paper* 171, London: International Institute for Strategic Studies, (1981); Idem., "Toward Nuclear Peace," in *Strategies for Managing Nuclear Proliferation: Economic and Political Issues*, ed. Dagobert L. Brito, Michael D. Intriligator, and Adele E. Wick (Lexington, MA: Lexington Books, 1983), 117–134; and Idem., "Why Iran Should Get the Bomb: Nuclear Balancing Would Mean Stability," *Foreign Affairs* 91, No. 4 (August 2012): 2–5.

national relations.[3] Indeed, he remains, according to a biographical account, "one of the most cited, and controversial, authors in the field of international relations."[4] He served as a President of the American Political Science Association (1987–1988). As a teacher Waltz influenced generations of students of international studies.[5]

In contrast to the proliferation optimists, proliferation pessimists contend that the dangers of nuclear proliferation are substantial and that growth in the number of countries with nuclear arsenals poses real risks to international peace and stability. Scott Sagan has taken a lead in representing this perspective, arguing that "more will be worse,"[6] although most other academic students of nuclear proliferation agree with him on this issue even if not accepting any or all of his arguments.

---

3. Waltz's best known works are *Man, the State, and War: a Theoretical Analysis* (New York: Columbia University Press, 1959), and *Theory of International Politics* (Reading, MA: Addison-Wesley Pub. Co., 1979). He is most closely associated with what has come to be called the neorealist view of international relations, as formally presented in *Theory of International Politics*. For a discussion of the importance of his work, see Robert O. Keohane, *Neorealism and Its Critics* (New York: Columbia University Press, 1986), 15–16.

4. Robert H. Lieshout, "Waltz, Kenneth (1924–)," in *Encyclopedia of Power*, ed. Keith Dowling (Thousand Oaks, California: Sage Publications, 2011), 701–702.

5. He was the Ford Professor of Political Science Emeritus at the University of California, Berkeley, but also taught at Columbia University and elsewhere during his long academic career. For a short biographical sketch, see *gsas.columbia.edu/news/kenneth-waltz,-theorist-of-international-relations,-dies-at-88/full*.

6. Dr. Scott Sagan is the Caroline S.G. Munro Professor of Political Science at Stanford University and a Senior Fellow at both the Center for International Security and Cooperation and the Freeman Spogli Institute. See cisac.fsi.stanford.edu/people/scott_d_sagan. He is a prominent scholar of nuclear issues, and has published *Moving Targets: Nuclear Strategy and National Security* (Princeton University Press, 1989) and *The Limits of Safety: Organizations, Accidents, and Nuclear Weapons* (Princeton University Press, 1993). The first articulation of his critique of Waltz's views was in Scott Douglas Sagan, "The Perils of Proliferation: Organization Theory, Deterrence Theory, and the Spread of Nuclear Weapons," *International Security* 18, No. 4, (Spring 1994): 66–107.

Waltz and Sagan have honed their disagreement in a short book, The Spread of Nuclear Weapons, widely used in the classroom to teach nuclear proliferation issues. First appearing in 1995, the two authors released revised versions in 2002 and 2013.[7]

The Nuclear Peace Hypothesis

At the center of the debate between the proliferation optimists and pessimists is what is sometimes called the nuclear peace hypothesis.[8] The thesis, first articulated in the months after the bombing of Hiroshima and Nagasaki, is an argument that the destructiveness of atomic weapons fundamentally alters international society by making warfare intolerable. In essence, the atomic bomb created a situation in which the means of warfare were incommensurate with the ends, such that it no longer made sense to contemplate general wars as a tool of policy. Bernard Brodie offered a stark statement of the concept in one of the seminal works of nuclear strategy.

> Thus far the chief purpose of our military establishment has been to win wars. From now on its chief purpose must be to avert them. It can have almost no other useful purpose.[9]

---

7. The version used to support this chapter is the 2002 edition, *The Spread of Nuclear Weapons: A Debate Renewed: With New Sections on India and Pakistan, Terrorism, and Missile Defense*, 2nd ed., (New York: W.W. Norton & Co., 2002). For critiques, see, Peter R. Lavoy, "The Strategic Consequences of Nuclear Proliferation: A Review Essay," *Security Studies* 4, No. 4, (1995): 695–753; David J. Karl, "Proliferation Pessimism and Emerging Nuclear Powers," *International Security* 21, No. 3 (1996): 87–119.

8. Some use different language to name the hypothesis. Robert Jervis, for example, called it the "nuclear revolution," in *The Meaning of the Nuclear Revolution: Statecraft and the Prospect of Armageddon* (Ithaca, NY: Cornell University Press, 1989).

9. Bernard Brodie, "Implications for Military Policy," in *The Absolute Weapon: Atomic Power and World Order* (New York: Harcourt, Brace and Company, 1946), 76.

Although Brodie came to modify his views, especially in his subsequent work on limited warfare, this 1946 statement is at the core of the argument offered by proliferation optimists.

Proponents of the nuclear peace hypothesis argue that the destructiveness of nuclear weapons makes national leaders reluctant to pursue military actions that might escalate into a nuclear exchange. From this perspective, there are few war objectives that could justify risking the death and destruction associated with a war fought using nuclear weapons. Some have argued that nuclear arsenals played a central role in creating the so-called "Long Peace" during the Cold War, a reference to the absence of significant armed conflict between the Soviet Union and the United States despite bitter enmity and mass arms build-ups.[10] Others also argue that nuclear weapons are responsible in part for the absence of major power wars in the past six decades.[11] While the nuclear peace hypothesis is contested by many, that debate will not be reviewed here.[12]

The focus of this paper is on a different issue, closely connected, that helps explain the indifference of policymakers to the Waltz argument: Why do U.S. policymakers—meaning government officials who have had positions of responsibility for such matters—overwhelmingly support nuclear nonproliferation efforts, irrespective of party or ideology or attitude towards nuclear weapons, even those who accept the tenets of the nuclear peace hypothesis? Or, to

---

10. John Lewis Gaddis, "The Long Peace: Elements of Stability in the Postwar International System," *International Security* 10, No. 4, (Spring 1986): 99–142.

11. Robert Rauchhaus, "Evaluating the Nuclear Peace Hypothesis," *Journal of Conflict Resolution* 53, No. 2, (April 2009): 258–277.

12. The criticisms come from multiple perspectives, as reflected in the essays found in Charles W. Kegley, editor, *The Long Postwar Peace: Contending Explanations and Projections* (New York: HarperCollins Publishers, 1991). Another version was offered by John Mueller, who contended that changing views of war, not the development and deployment of nuclear weapons, was responsible for the absence of major power wars. See, John E. Mueller, *Retreat from Doomsday: The Obsolescence of Major War* (New York: Basic Books, 1989).

reframe the question in the context of the academic debate: why are policymakers overwhelmingly inclined towards proliferation pessimism?

Nuclear Optimism, Proliferation Optimism, and Proliferation Relativism

As a starting point, there are important differences between "nuclear optimism," the concept that nuclear weapons can prevent wars with limited danger of nuclear use, and "proliferation optimism," the decidedly different argument that the spread of nuclear weapons is not accompanied by an increase in the dangers that they pose. Sagan, for example, implicitly assumes that those who accept the nuclear peace hypothesis also favor proliferation, meaning that "nuclear optimists" are the same as "proliferation optimists."[13] That is a doubtful conclusion. A "proliferation optimist" inevitably will be a "nuclear optimist," believing that the spread of nuclear weapons will favor international peace, but a "nuclear optimist" need not be a "proliferation optimist." Indeed, as will become evident, many "nuclear optimists" are "proliferation pessimists," and even those sometimes classified as "proliferation optimists" often are highly selective in their optimism.

Distinguishing the "proliferation optimist" from what Peter Lavoy has called the "proliferation relativist" is critically important to understanding different views regarding the merits of nuclear proliferation.[14] Some academics considered "proliferation optimists" hold positions radically different from the one advanced by Waltz, perhaps accepting the "nuclear peace hypothesis" but not necessarily considering all nuclear proliferation beneficial.

---

13. Sagan, "The Perils of Proliferation: Organization Theory, Deterrence Theory, and the Spread of Nuclear Weapons."

14. Lavoy, "The Strategic Consequences of Nuclear Proliferation: A Review Essay."

John Mearsheimer, often identified as a "proliferation optimist,"[15] is better characterized as a "proliferation relativist." Rather than advocating "more is better," he has supported selective proliferation. Thus, in the early 1990s he argued that Ukraine should retain the nuclear weapons that it acquired with the disintegration of the Soviet Union. In his view, international stability was enhanced when the major European powers had nuclear weapons.[16] He also made clear that smaller countries should not get them at all. According to Mearsheimer, "Nuclear proliferation does not axiomatically promote peace and can in some cases even cause war."[17] While it is beyond the scope of this paper to assess the theoretical foundations of their world views, it is perhaps worth noting that Waltz and Mearsheimer share fundamentally similar conceptions of the international system, but still seem to have rather different views on the role of nuclear weapons. While Waltz is a strong advocate of the nuclear peace hypothesis, Mearsheimer appears less convinced that a nuclear revolution has changed the fundamentals of international relations.[18]

---

15. Joel Marks, "Nuclear Prudence or Nuclear Psychosis? Structural Realism and the Proliferation of Nuclear Weapons," *Global Change, Peace & Security* 21, No. 3 (2009): 325–340; and Sagan, "The Perils of Proliferation: Organization Theory, Deterrence Theory, and the Spread of Nuclear Weapons," 66–67.

16. John J. Mearsheimer, "The Case for a Ukrainian Nuclear Deterrent," *Foreign Affairs* 72, No. 3, (Summer 1993): 50–66; and Idem., "Back to the Future: Instability in Europe after the Cold War," *International Security* 15, No. 1, (Summer 1990): 5–56.

17. Idem., "The Case for a Ukrainian Nuclear Deterrent," 51.

18. An overview that distinguishes Waltz and Mearsheimer is John J. Mearsheimer, "Structural Realism," in *International Relations Theories: Discipline and Diversity,* ed. Tim Dunne, Milja Kurki, and Steve Smith (Oxford: Oxford University Press, 2006), 71–88. For attempts to understand their contrasting views of nuclear weapons, see, Marks, "Nuclear Prudence or Nuclear Psychosis?"; and Zanvyl Krieger and Ariel Ilan Roth, "Nuclear Weapons in Neo-Realist Theory," International Studies Review, Vol. 9, No. 3, Autumn 2007, 369–384.

Indeed, what is striking is that most so-called "proliferation optimists" are actually "proliferation relativists." Bruce Bueno de Mesquita wrote about the benefits of "selective" proliferation, arguing that in some instances nuclear proliferation was beneficial even as he accepted that it could have profoundly negative consequences in other cases.[19] Similarly, Dagobert L. Brito and Michael D. Intriligator, also often considered "proliferation optimists," actually make a rather different argument. While they contend that increasing the number of nuclear weapons states may or may not increase the risks of deliberate nuclear war, more proliferation does increase the prospects for "nuclear war due to accidents, irrationality, or political instability."[20] While more sanguine than many others, it would be a stretch to identify such views as optimistic.

The distinction between "proliferation optimism" and "proliferation relativism" is critical to understanding how Waltz's views of proliferation fit within the broader spectrum of alternative perspectives of the challenges posed by the spread of nuclear weapons. Similarly, as will become clear, support for the nuclear peace hypothesis, what might be termed "nuclear optimism," does not necessarily lead to "proliferation optimism." It is these distinctions that help explain why policymakers, even those who may accept the "nuclear peace hypothesis," dismiss Waltz and his optimistic views on nuclear proliferation.

Proliferation Optimism

What are the arguments justifying proliferation optimism? The following paragraphs summarize the key elements of Waltz's argu-

---

19. Bruce Bueno de Mesquita and William H. Riker, "An Assessment of the Merits of Selective Nuclear Proliferation," *Journal of Conflict Resolution* 26, No. 2, (June 1982): 283–306.

20. Dagobert L. Brito and Michael D. Intriligator, "Proliferation and the Probability of War: A Cardinality Theorem," *Journal of Conflict Resolution* 40, No. 1, (March 1996): 212.

ment, ignoring some important points he makes for purposes of completeness but are relatively tangential to his core argument.

Underlying Waltz's argument are several assumptions that derived from his views of how the international system operates and his adherence to the nuclear peace hypothesis. First, he argued, "Deterrent balances are inherently stable."[21] He contended that nuclear deterrence did not depend on the size of nuclear arsenals, because there was little incentive to acquire more weapons once a country "securely established" its deterrent.[22] Second, he argued that the resulting deterrence stability is insensitive to the character of regimes, essentially arguing that all states and all possible national leaders can be trusted to use their nuclear forces with prudence. For that reason, he argued that Libya under Muammar Qaddafi, Uganda under Idi Amin, or Iraq under Saddam Hussein would behave similarly to a United States under Dwight Eisenhower or a Soviet Union under Mikhail Gorbachev. Indeed, he even argued that a nuclear-armed Europe would have moderated the behavior of Adolf Hitler.[23] Third, Waltz believed that extremely small nuclear arsenals, perhaps consisting of only a handful of weapons, can establish a credible deterrent. Based on this belief, he argued that Israel could deter Libya with only two weapons, one for Benghazi and one for Tripoli, while Libya need only possess enough weapons to destroy Tel Aviv and Haifa in return.[24]

Waltz believed that establishing the conditions for stable deterrence relationships was not difficult, although he did recognize that it was not necessarily automatic. First, he accepted that a slow pace of

---

21. Sagan and Waltz, 30.

22. Ibid., 31. Thus, Waltz notes that the United Kingdom and France built small arsenals to deter the Soviet Union, compared with the massive—and to Waltz totally unnecessary—U.S. nuclear force.

23. Ibid., 13–14, 28–29.

24. Ibid., 21–22. This assumes, of course, that the appropriate target is a city, which has been a source of contention in U.S. nuclear strategy since the 1950s.

proliferation was essential, because "rapid changes in international conditions can be unsettling."[25] However, he rejected the concept of proliferation cascades, and so did not see this as a significant concern. From his perspective, only a few non-nuclear states will be an interest in acquiring a nuclear arsenal at any given point in time.

Second, Waltz also recognized that countries must create nuclear capabilities that could reliably mount retaliatory attacks. Waltz specified several requirements for such a force. It must be able to survive attack and have the means to deliver the surviving weapons. He saw these requirements as important primarily because they obviated the need for a launch-on-warning or under attack capability. Also essential was a robust command and control system, primarily to prevent unauthorized use.[26] Waltz was convinced that it was not hard to satisfy these requirements, even for a small country with a limited nuclear arsenal. Hiding weapons and protecting them (and their delivery systems) from attack was simple to achieve in his view and the rudimentary command and control systems required were within the reach of even the smallest of powers.[27]

He applied similar thinking to both the U.S.-Soviet nuclear balance and the U.S. nuclear arsenal. As a result, he rejected the core precepts that guided U.S. nuclear policy during the Cold War, whether it was the complicated interactions between deterrence and nuclear warfighting in Department of Defense nuclear planning or the force structure that he saw as grossly oversized.[28] Thus, Waltz adopted theoretical constructs that are in specific opposition to past

---

25. Ibid., 3, 42–43. If deterrence is inherently stable, Waltz does not explain why the speed of the spread of nuclear weapons should make a difference.

26. Ibid., 20.

27. Ibid., 21; and Kenneth Neal Waltz, "A Reply," *Security Studies* 4, No. 4, (Summer 1995): 802–805.

28. Kenneth Neal Waltz, "Nuclear Myths and Political Realities," *American Political Science Review* 84, No. 3, (September 1990): 731–745.

and present U.S. nuclear policy, strategy, and operations.[29] It is that divergence that lies at the core of the disagreement between the perspectives of Washington policymakers and the academic theoretician.

Policymakers and Nuclear Nonproliferation

During the past seven decades, U.S. policymakers worried about the prospects for the proliferation of nuclear weapons, even if ultimately other considerations took precedence. This perspective is reflected in the observation of the Congressional Commission on the Strategic Posture of the United States that, since the beginning, U.S. nuclear policy has had two "imperatives": the requirement for a strong nuclear deterrent and reliance on arms control and nonproliferation measures.[30] This juxtaposition is significant, given that this commission was comprised of men and women selected to represent the views of Washington's political elite, including amongst its members former U.S. government policymakers in the U.S. government who had been involved in the development or implementation of strategic nuclear policy.

Every U.S. president since the detonation of the first atomic bomb has articulated policies consistent with this dual vision, although some had little confidence in nonproliferation and can be justifiably criticized for that. Official policy from the dawn of the atomic age called for constraints on nuclear weapons, starting in the months after Hiroshima, when the leaders of the Western countries

---

29. Here I refer not to former policymakers, who often adopt positions rather different than the ones they propounded while in office, but only to the views of those in positions of responsibility, except when their positions out of government seem to comport with the positions they held while in government.

30. Congressional Commission on the Strategic Posture of the United States, *America's Strategic Posture: The Final Report of the Congressional Commission on the Strategic Posture of the United States* (Washington, DC: United States Institute of Peace Press, 2009), 5.

announced what became the Baruch Plan, which called for international, not national, control of nuclear materials. Consistent with
this vision, the Atomic Energy Act prohibited transfers of nuclear
materials and weapons information even to our British and Canadian allies, who had contributed so substantially to the Manhattan
Project. As former U.S. Secretary of State Dean Acheson asserted
in 1966, perhaps with some overstatement, "The United States believed—and this is something that it is easy for everyone in the
world to forget—that even one nuclear power was too many, and
immediately after World War II we sought to remove nuclear energy from the military field."[31]

In the subsequent two decades, until negotiation of the 1969 Nuclear Nonproliferation Treaty, most policymakers at best tolerated
nuclear proliferation and only a few actively thought it a good
thing.[32] Even U.S. President Dwight Eisenhower, often criticized
by the nonproliferation community for his role in spreading nuclear technology through the Atoms for Peace program, opposed
nuclear proliferation and apparently thought that his policies were
consistent with that objective.[33]

In some respects, this consensus in policymaking circles is surprising. On other nuclear matters there often was widespread disagree-

31. Statement by Secretary of State Rusk to the Joint Committee on Atomic
Energy: Nonproliferation of Nuclear Weapons, February 23, 1966, *Documents
on Disarmament, 1966*, (Washington, D.C.: Arms Control and Disarmament
Agency, 1967), 41-49.

32. For a discussion of views during the Kennedy, Johnson, and early Nixon administrations, see Francis J. Gavin, "Blasts from the Past: Proliferation Lessons
from the 1960s," *International Security* 29, No. 3, (Winter 2004-05): 100–135.

33. Eisenhower advocated an International Atomic Energy Agency and a Comprehensive Nuclear-Test-Ban Treaty in part to develop barriers against proliferation, according to George Bunn, "U.S. Non-Proliferation Policy," in *Arms
Control for the Late Sixties* (Princeton, N.J.: Van Nostrand, 1967), 151. For a
not unsympathetic critique of Eisenhower's nonproliferation record, see Shane
Maddock, "The Fourth Country Problem: Eisenhower's Nuclear Nonproliferation Policy," *Presidential Studies Quarterly* 28, No. 3, (Summer 1998): 553–572.

ment. Yet, it is evident that many people who firmly believed in the strength of deterrence, and probably believed that nuclear weapons played an important, perhaps even decisive role, in maintaining global peace during the Cold War, also fought to prevent the further proliferation of nuclear weapons. Amongst the primary intellectual figures of U.S. nuclear deterrence strategy were individuals closely associated with nuclear nonproliferation policies, such as Albert Wohlstetter.[34]

How do we know what they think? While there are no opinion surveys to prove the point, there is little doubt that the overwhelming majority of U.S. senior national security executives during the nuclear age opposed the proliferation of nuclear weapons, even when friendly countries were involved. We know this in several ways. First, we know what they have said and written. Few have adopted a position consistent with the proliferation optimists,[35] while most have viewed proliferation as a serious national security challenge.[36]

---

34. Wohlstetter is best known for his seminal study, Albert Wohlstetter, "The Delicate Balance of Terror," *Foreign Affairs* 37, No. 2, (January 1959): 211–234. Others who expressed concern about nuclear proliferation were such prominent figures as Bernard Brodie, Fred Iklé, Arnold Kramish, and James Schlesinger, albeit in differing degrees. Consider the following observations in Bernard Brodie, Charles J. Hitch, and Andrew W. Marshall, *The Next Ten Years* (Santa Monica, California: RAND, 1954), 16–17.

> This is likely to restore greater importance to other nations vis-à-vis the U.S. and U.S.S.R. and might significantly alter the present bi-polar distribution of power. Whether wider distribution of power will be in the U.S. interest or will enhance the chances of world peace is disputable. Certainly the problems of national security in a multi-polar world with asymptotic weapons would be very different in character.

35. A rare example of a nuclear proliferation proponent was General Curtis LeMay, who lambasted nonproliferation policies after he retired from the military. Curtis E. LeMay and Dale O. Smith, *America Is in Danger* (New York: Funk & Wagnalls, 1968), 186–221.

36. James Schlesinger, "The Impact of Nuclear Weapons on History," *Washington Quarterly* 16, No. 4, (August 1993): 5–12; Harold Brown, "New Nuclear

Perhaps more significantly, we also can review what policies they have advocated and implemented.

What are some of the considerations that make most U.S. policy-makers nuclear proliferation pessimists? This paper explores five such considerations: (1) widespread ambivalence about nuclear weapons; (2) concerns about the stability of nuclear deterrence; (3) the challenges that nuclear proliferation pose to the U.S. global position; (4) the risks of nuclear terrorism resulting from loss of control of nuclear arsenals in failed states; and, (5) the complexity of crisis management. Other considerations could be added to this list, such as worries about the quality of intelligence concerning foreign nuclear programs or the ability of any country to ensure the safe operation of nuclear arsenals.[37]

U.S. Ambivalence Towards Nuclear Weapons

In contrast to Waltz's comfort with a nuclear-armed world, U.S. government officials, especially at the more senior levels, often are more ambivalent. They recognize the strategic value of nuclear weapons, but also worry about their destructiveness and the dangers associated with their possession and potential use. This view is aptly summarized in another of Brodie's writings.

> All civilized people share in greater or less degree
> the desire to put the "nuclear genie back in the bot-
> tle" (though, like the classical genie, it has also done
> some useful service—such as critically reducing the
> probability of war between the United States and

Realities," *Washington Quarterly* 31, No. 1, (Winter 2007): 7–22; and Carl Kaysen, Robert S. McNamara, and George W. Rathjens, "Nuclear Weapons After the Cold War," *Foreign Affairs* 70, No. 4, (Fall 1991): 95–110.

37. This is a particular concern of Sagan's, as summarized in Sagan and Waltz, *The Spread of Nuclear Weapons: A Debate Renewed: With New Sections on India and Pakistan, Terrorism, and Missile Defense*, 72–82.

the Soviet Union).[38]

More important, most U.S. presidents have had such conflicted views. Almost none have been completely comfortable with nuclear weapons; many sought to limit or eliminate them. The views of U.S. President Barack Obama on the ultimate need to create a world without nuclear weapons, sometimes articulated as a new departure, also reflect the publicly and privately expressed opinions of most of his predecessors. Famously, U.S. President Ronald Reagan was willing to discuss complete elimination of nuclear weapons during the October 1986 Reykjavik Summit, declaring, "It would be fine with me if we eliminated all nuclear weapons."[39] He justified his support for the Strategic Defense Initiative by talking of "rendering these nuclear weapons impotent and obsolete."[40] Even President Eisenhower, who of all the presidents was most attracted to the benefits provided by nuclear deterrence, often expressed both his fears of their destructive powers and the ultimate need to eliminate them.[41]

Striving for the ultimate elimination of nuclear weapons has never been seen as necessarily incompatible with acceptance of nuclear deterrence in the shorter term. Indeed, since the dawn of the nuclear

---

38. Bernard Brodie, "The McNamara Phenomenon," *World Politics* 17, No. 4, (July 1965): 680.

39. The passage is on page 11 of the official U.S. Memorandum of Conversation, October 11, 1986, in Svetlana Savranskaya and Thomas Blanton, eds., "The Reykjavik File: Previously Secret U.S. and Soviet Documents on the 1986 Reagan-Gorbachev Summit," Electronic Briefing Book 203, Document 11, National Security Archive, October 13, 2006, available from *www2.gwu.edu/~nsarchiv/ NSAEBB/NSAEBB203/Document11.pdf.*

40. Ronald Reagan, "Address to the Nation on Defense and National Security," March 23, 1983. Online by Gerhard Peters and John T. Woolley, eds., The American Presidency Project, available from *www.presidency.ucsb.edu/ ws/?pid=41093.*

41. David S. Patterson, "President Eisenhower and Arms Control," *Peace & Change* 11, No. 3, (Summer 1986), 3–24.

age official U.S. policy has been the ultimate elimination of nuclear weapons, even if only in the context of general and complete disarmament. This incongruity is well demonstrated with the varying views of nuclear weapons evident among the so-called "Gang of Four," the four former U.S. senior statesmen (Henry Kissinger, Sam Nunn, William Perry, and George Shultz) who called for the revitalization of efforts to eliminate nuclear weapons.[42] While often viewed as a radical break from the past, the differences are actually less obvious. All support maintaining a reliable nuclear deterrent.[43]

Such skepticism does not comport well with "more is better." Why actively promote the spread of a weapon that you believe ultimately should be banned? At the very least, this helps explain the ambivalence that often attended thinking about such matters when the issue of nuclear assistance arose.

Many in the United States argue that nuclear weapons are essential only to deter other nuclear weapons.[44] This is not official U.S. national policy, although the 2010 Nuclear Posture Review noted a trend to move in that direction.

> The United States will continue to strengthen conventional capabilities and reduce the role of nuclear

---

42. George P. Shultz, et al., "A World Free of Nuclear Weapons," *Wall Street Journal*, January 4, 2007.

43. All four authors of the original editorial have supported the recommendations of the Congressional Commission on the Strategic Posture of the United States, which was co-chaired by Perry. See, George P. Shultz, et al., "How to Protect Our Nuclear Deterrent," *Wall Street Journal*, January 20, 2010, A17; and also see, America's Strategic Posture: The Final Report of the Congressional Commission on the Strategic Posture of the United States. Kissinger clearly articulates the need for a robust deterrent in Henry A. Kissinger and Brent Scowcroft, "Strategic Stability in Today's Nuclear World," *Washington Post*, April 23, 2012, A13.

44. McGeorge Bundy, "The Bishops and the Bomb," *New York Review of Books*, June 16, 1983; and Robert S. McNamara, "The Military Role of Nuclear Weapons: Perceptions and Misperceptions," *Foreign Affairs* 62, No. 1, (Fall 1983): 59–80.

> weapons in deterring non-nuclear attacks, with the
> objective of making deterrence of nuclear attack on
> the United States or our allies and partners the sole
> purpose of U.S. nuclear weapons.[45]

This reflected a long standing effort to reduce the role of nuclear weapons by providing the president with conventional options. The United States has developed formidable advanced conventional military capabilities, involving precision strike munitions, sophisticated intelligence, surveillance, and reconnaissance (ISR) systems, and complex command and control systems. Part of the impetus for the development of these systems was a desire to raise the threshold for use of nuclear weapons.[46] The United States currently can employ conventional forces to accomplish military objectives requiring nuclear weapons in an earlier era. For this reason, the United States does not rely on nuclear weapons to the same extent as other powers (and certainly not as much as Russia, which requires them even for defense against large-scale conventional attacks). From this perspective, so argues Harold Brown, the former Secretary of Defense who did much to encourage the development of such capabilities, the United States would benefit more than any other power should nuclear weapons totally disappear today.[47] While many of his peers would disagree with his ultimate conclusion, few would disagree that during the past four decades the United States systematically worked to acquire conventional weapons capabilities motivated in part by a desire to reduce requirements for nuclear weapons.[48]

---

45. Department of Defense, *Nuclear Posture Review Report* (Washington, D.C., April 2010), ix.

46. Commission on Integrated Long-Term Strategy, *Discriminate Deterrence* (Washington, D.C.: Department of Defense, 1987), 8.

47. Brown, "New Nuclear Realities," 16–17.

48. This trend is reviewed in Barry D. Watts, *Nuclear-Conventional Firebreaks and the Nuclear Taboo* (Washington, D.C.: Center for Strategic and Budgetary Assessments, 2013).

The Difficulties of Maintaining a Deterrent

Policymakers and analysts intimately involved with U.S. nuclear weapons policy were not sanguine about the ease of maintaining deterrence relationships. Indeed, most clearly accepted the view articulated by Albert Wohlstetter in the late 1950s when writing about the initial efforts to create a stable deterrent in a world populated both by thermonuclear weapons and intercontinental ballistic missiles: "Deterrence in the 1960's is neither assured nor impossible but will be the product of sustained intelligent effort and hard choices."[49] As Wohlstetter argued in his seminal article, "The Delicate Balance of Terror," ensuring the survivability of a nuclear deterrent is complex and costly.[50]

From the perspective of practitioners of nuclear strategy, Waltz ignored the harsh realities of nuclear strategy development and implementation. Consider the comments of David Rosenberg about his seminal article on early U.S. nuclear strategy.

> [This article] addresses nuclear strategy not as an exercise in conceptualization, but rather as a complex endeavor, partly intellectual and partly bureaucratic. It focuses specifically on the strategic and operational planning process for nuclear war—where concepts were translated into damage criteria, tactics, targets, and weapons—and how that process related to dynamics such as high policy guidance, strategic theory, and technological development which should have served to control and regulate it.[51]

---

49. Charles J. Hitch and Roland N. McKean, *The Economics of Defense in the Nuclear Age, Vol. R-346 (*Santa Monica, California: RAND, 1960), 334.

50. Wohlstetter, "The Delicate Balance of Terror."

51. David Alan Rosenberg, "The Origins of Overkill: Nuclear Weapons and American Strategy, 1945-1960," *International Security* 7, No. 4 (Spring 1983): 8.

In contrast, Waltz views deterrence "as an exercise in conceptual-ization." Consider the difference between Waltz's views and those of practitioners on two issues: ensuring the survivability of nuclear forces and evaluating the utility of small nuclear forces.

Waltz contended that any state possessing nuclear weapons will take effective steps to ensure the survivability of its arsenal. That was not the sense of Wohlstetter and his RAND colleagues, who believed that the U.S. Strategic Air Command, focused largely on its own retaliatory capabilities, largely ignored its own vulnerabili-ty to a surprise attack.[52] Waltz discounted such concerns by arguing that they were misguided, claiming that during the Cuban Missile Crisis the United States was deterred by a relatively small Soviet nuclear force (perhaps limited to 60-70 weapons capable of reach-ing the United States, contrasting with 2,000 weapons that we had that could strike the Soviet Union).[53] However, Waltz also appar-ently was quite comfortable retaliating against cities in response to counterforce attacks, a position that many American nuclear strate-gists found unpalatable.[54]

We also have some evidence to suggest that small nuclear powers have difficulty in maintaining the survivability of their nuclear ar-senal. The South Africans stored their entire arsenal of six bombs in a single building vulnerable even to conventional air strikes, protected only by their ability to keep its location a secret.[55] While one presumes that these weapons would have been dispersed in the event of a crisis, we are told that the Soviet Union considered preemptive attacks against the nascent South African program.[56]

---

52. Bernard Brodie, *War and Politics* (New York: Macmillan, 1973), 380

53. Waltz, "Nuclear Myths and Political Realities," 734.

54. Rosenberg, 35–36, 58–60.

55. David Albright, "South Africa and the Affordable Bomb," *Bulletin of the Atomic Scientists* 50, No. 4 (July/August 1994), 43–44.

56. Ibid., 42.

Admittedly, we do not know if the Soviets knew the location of those weapons, but given known penetrations of the South African military establishment, it is possible that they did.[57]

The Pakistanis certainly seem to worry about the survivability of their nuclear arsenal, concerned both that the United States might attempt to seize control of it and that India might preemptively neutralize their deterrent forces by destroying the weapons still in their storage bunkers. Indeed, experts on Pakistan's nuclear forces appear to believe that its arsenal will be dispersed in the event of a crisis due to concerns about its survivability.[58] Clearly, the Pakistanis are not confident about the survivability of their arsenal under routine circumstances.

It is surprising that Waltz is so confident about the survivability of small nuclear arsenals. The argument rests largely on the confidence that any country can have that its greatest secrets have not been compromised. In the case of South Africa, knowledge of one location would have permitted a decisive disarming attack. Even in the case of Pakistan, with its larger and more sophisticated force structure, weapons apparently are stored at only six to 12 sites, according to at least one account.[59] Much can be done to reduce the vulnerability of such a force by relying on hardened bunkers or underground facilities, but that transforms the arsenal into something

---

57. Ibid., mentions the role of Dieter Gerhardt, a South African naval officer who spied for the Soviets. The available evidence suggests that Gerhardt had access to details of the South African nuclear program, and it appears he gave that information to the Soviet Union. According to Gerhardt, the Soviets considered a strike against the South African enrichment facility in 1976. None of the available accounts indicates whether Gerhardt also knew of the location of the South African nuclear arsenal before his arrest in 1983. However, the storage facility was operational in 1981, so it is at least possible that he might have provided that information to the Soviets as well.

58. Vipin Narang, "Posturing for Peace? Pakistan's Nuclear Postures and South Asian Stability," *International Security* 34, No. 3 (Winter 2009-10): 38–78.

59, Vipin Narang, "Posturing for Peace? Pakistan's Nuclear Postures and South Asian Stability," *International Security* 34, No. 3 (Winter 2009-10) 38–78.

that begins to look like a small version of a major power nuclear infrastructure.

As has been noted, Waltz argues that small nuclear forces can satisfy the requirements for a secure deterrent, contrasting the small arsenals of France and the United Kingdom with the vastly larger U.S. force structure. He seems to imply that the leaders of those two European countries believed that their arsenals comprised a self-sufficient deterrent to Soviet nuclear threats. Yet, the reality is that both countries saw their nuclear deterrent only in the U.S. context, not as totally isolated and independent forces. The British integrated their nuclear forces into a North Atlantic Treaty Organization (NATO) theater and a U.S. strategic response, while the French strategy focused heavily on manipulation of U.S. responses.[60]

Clearly, those who had to take responsibility for sustaining the U.S. deterrent were far less confident than Waltz about strategic stability. Indeed, during the decades that followed publication of Wohlstetter's article, concerns about strategic stability were a constant, irrespective of administration. Whether addressing the central strategic balance between the Soviet Union and the United States, or the NATO-Warsaw Pact regional balance in Europe, U.S. policymakers found nothing simple or easy about the process of generating and sustaining a credible deterrent.

Ultimately, Waltz's views matter rather less than the perspectives of several generations of practitioners who had rather different views

---

60. French nuclear strategy and its ties to the American nuclear arsenal are reviewed in Bruno Tertrais, "Destruction Assurée: The Origins and Development of French Nuclear Strategy, 1945-81," in Henry Sokoloski, ed., *Getting MAD: Nuclear Mutual Assured Destruction, Its Origins and Practice* (Carlisle, PA: Strategic Studies Institute, 2004), 51–122, available from *www.npolicy.org/books/Getting_MAD/Ch2_Tertrais.pdf*; and R. H. Ullman, "The Covert French Connection," *Foreign Policy*, No. 75 (Summer 1989): 3–33. The earliest British nuclear strategy documents tied their deterrent to the United States, according to John Simpson, "British Nuclear Weapon Stockpiles, 1953–78: A Commentary on Technical and Political Drivers," *The RUSI Journal* 156, no. 5 (2011): 74–83.

on deterrence. For those responsible for the lives of tens, perhaps hundreds, of millions of people, it is perhaps not surprising that they would be less inclined to take for granted the inherent stability of deterrence or that they might be less than comfortable with the argument that we should view with complacence the nuclear postures of other countries.

Challenging U.S. Dominance

Many in Washington opposed nuclear weapons programs because the proliferation of nuclear weapons would undermine U.S. political and military power. President Eisenhower apparently believed that the United States would benefit more from the elimination of nuclear weapons than the Soviet Union, given his confidence in U.S. economic and industrial strength.[61] As a future Secretary of Defense, James Schlesinger, would note in the late 1960s, "Further nuclear spread would lead to a reduction of the relative influence of the United States on the world scene."[62] Secretary of State Dean Rusk made it a generalized principle when he told a Soviet diplomat in 1963, "It was almost axiomatic that no nuclear power has any interest in seeing others become nuclear powers."[63]

The most obvious point about nuclear proliferation is that it may strengthen adversaries and weaken U.S. responses to their aggressive moves. Once it became clear in the 1950s that nuclear weapons, even when possessed in overwhelming numbers, could not prevent

---

61. Patterson, "President Eisenhower and Arms Control."

62. James Schlesinger, "The Strategic Consequences of Nuclear Proliferation," in *Arms Control for the Late Sixties* (Princeton, N.J.: Van Nostrand, 1967), 175. Schlesinger attributed the thought to William C. Foster, Arms Control and Disarmament Agency Director.

63. Memorandum of Conversation, January 10, 1963, U.S. Department of State, *Foreign Relations of the United States, 1961-1963: Arms Control and Disarmament, Volume 7* (Washington, D.C.: U.S. Government Printing Office, 1995), 630-631.

uses of conventional weapons peripheral to the core interests of the United States, U.S. policymakers had to worry that a nuclear umbrella could shield destabilizing actions by hostile countries, even if we did not fear use of nuclear weapons. This was one of the concerns that arose from consideration of China's acquisition of nuclear weapons,[64] and it has been a recurring theme in connection with lesser powers, such as Iran, Iraq, Libya, and North Korea, openly hostile to U.S. interests, who might strive to use a nuclear arsenal to undermine U.S. influence and interests.

Even more intriguing is the ambivalence or hostility of the United States towards the acquisition of nuclear weapons by close allies. U.S. theater nuclear weapons policy in Europe was calibrated to reduce incentives for NATO and even non-NATO countries to acquire their own independent nuclear deterrent. Although the British had been closely involved with the original Manhattan Project, it took time for the U.S. political establishment to accept Britain's nuclear status and even longer to develop the close ties that eventually emerged between the two country's nuclear programs.[65]

During the late 1950s and early 1960s, some U.S. government officials thought that the United States benefited from acquisition of nuclear weapons by allies. Thus, in 1955 President Eisenhower asked Harold Stassen to undertake arms control negotiations with the Soviet Union. Initially, Stassen was skeptical about the prospects for nuclear nonproliferation, but changed his views after concluding it was a possible area of diplomatic collaboration with the Soviet Union. However, some Defense Department officials strongly opposed his efforts in part because they thought it would be to the U.S. advantage if France and Japan had nuclear weap-

---

64. William Burr and Jeffrey T. Richelson, "Whether to 'Strangle the Baby in the Cradle': The United States and the Chinese Nuclear Program, 1960-64," *International Security* 25, No. 3 (Winter 2000-01): 54–99.

65. Simpson, "British Nuclear Weapon Stockpiles, 1953–78."

ons.[66]

Days after the first Chinese nuclear test in 1964, U.S. President Lyndon Johnson established the Gilpatric Committee to review nuclear nonproliferation policy. The Committee discovered that the Defense Department no longer opposed nuclear nonproliferation, but that the State Department was strongly opposed to any policy that would overtly prevent certain U.S. allies from retaining the right to acquire nuclear weapons. In particular, some senior State Department officials at the time believed that U.S. alliance relations depended on creation of the Multi-Lateral Force (MLF), which would have given NATO allies direct access to nuclear weapons. Moreover, some senior State Department officials believed that we would undermine alliance relationships if we tried to deny Germany and Japan the right to acquire nuclear weapons.[67] However, the MLF never became a reality, and the president never accepted the State Department's hostility towards nuclear nonproliferation.

Over time, U.S. officials came to worry that allied nuclear weapons capabilities posed dangers to the U.S.-Soviet deterrence relationship. And, although it may be true that the United States provided assistance to the French nuclear weapons program,[68] it is equally clear that from the French perspective the United States was a huge obstacle in its development of an independent nuclear capability in the 1950s and 1960s.[69] Indeed, one rationale for the French nuclear program was to deny the United States independence of action in responding to the Soviet Union. Paris wanted to ensure that the United States took into account French security interests. Unfortunately, it also complicated NATO nuclear weapons planning. For example, the United States worried that efforts to keep a conflict

66. See, Maddock, 557–558.

67. Gavin, "Blasts from the Past: Proliferation Lessons from the 1960s."

68. Ullman, "The Covert French Connection."

69. Tertrais, "Destruction Assurée: The Origins and Development of French Nuclear Strategy, 1945-81."

limited might be derailed by French nuclear attacks against attacking Soviet ground forces in Central Europe.[70]

Ultimately the United States exerted considerable pressure on other friendly countries during the Cold War, such as South Korea and Taiwan, to constrain their nuclear ambitions, and worked during the 1950s and 1960s—admittedly not always pursued consistently— to limit the spread of nuclear weapons in Europe.[71]

Interestingly, Waltz at one point concedes such worries about the negative impact of nuclear proliferation by accepting that "limitation of America's policy choices has been one of the costs" of proliferation, but finds the benefits he sees in limiting adversary choices well worth that price.[72] It is perhaps unsurprising that those in Washington responsible for U.S. policy are less sanguine about the costs of permitting reductions in U.S. relative power.

Failed States and Nuclear Terrorism

A major concern for U.S. policymakers, especially since 9/11, has been the danger that nuclear weapons may fall into the hands of terrorists. While some analysts believe that the threat of nuclear terrorism is overstated, and others that it is irrelevant, the concern is not new.[73] The national security community in the United States

---

70. Ullman, "The Covert French Connection."

71. The list of NATO countries and European neutrals that abandoned nuclear weapons programs—albeit, many nascent at best—is long: Germany, Italy, Netherlands, Norway, Sweden, Switzerland, and Yugoslavia. See, Ariel Levite, "Never Say Never Again: Nuclear Reversal Revisited," *International Security* 27, No. 3 (Winter 2002-03): 62.

72. Waltz, "A Reply," 805. However, he also asserted that focusing on nuclear nonproliferation required the United States to pay an unnecessary diplomatic price using resources better devoted to other, more important concerns. See Sagan and Waltz, *The Spread of Nuclear Weapons: A Debate Renewed*, 42.

73.. Brian Michael Jenkins, *Will Terrorists Go Nuclear?* (Amherst, N.Y.: Pro-

has discussed the issue since at least the early 1970s, and worries about nuclear terrorism have motivated much activity intended to control fissile material.[74]

For many, the most likely way in which this could happen is as a result of political instability in a nuclear-armed country. This problem first emerged as a concern in the early 1990s with the collapse of the Soviet Union at the end of the Cold War. At that time, the Soviet nuclear arsenal was divided between four countries, and security for protecting weapons and fissile material was uncertain at best. In addition to taking steps to ensure consolidation of the weapons under the sole control of Russia, the United States funded a variety of programs intended to prevent loss of weapons, fissile material, or critical technology.[75]

Today the primary concern is that the political collapse of North Korea or Pakistan could lead to a loss of control and the subsequent acquisition of nuclear weapons by a terrorist group. This is particularly worrying in the case of Pakistan, given the presence and strength of terrorist groups in that country that might be inclined to use such weapons.[76] President Obama has made the risks of terrorist acquisition of nuclear weapons a central concern of his administration. As he argued in his 2009 Prague speech, "This is the

---

metheus Books, 2008); and John E. Mueller, *Overblown: How Politicians and the Terrorism Industry Inflate National Security Threats, and Why We Believe Them* (New York: Free Press, 2006).

74. Mason Willrich and Theodore B. Taylor, *Nuclear Theft: Risks and Safeguards; a Report to the Energy Policy Project of the Ford Foundation* (Cambridge, MA: Ballinger Pub. Co., 1974), 114–116, provides an early discussion.

75. Graham T. Allison, et al., *Avoiding Nuclear Anarchy: Containing the Threat of Loose Russian Nuclear Weapons and Fissile Material, Vol. 12* (Cambridge, MA: MIT Press, 1996).

76. Thomas Donnelly, "Bad Options: Or How I Stopped Worrying and Learned to Live with Loose Nukes," in Henry D. Sokolski, ed., *Pakistan's Nuclear Future: Worries Beyond War* (Carlisle, PA: Strategic Studies Institute, 2008) 347–368.

most immediate and extreme threat to global security."[77] While the rationale differed, U.S. President George W. Bush also considered nuclear terrorism as one of his top national security challenges.[78]

Recent developments in Syria also illustrate this point. The Syrians amassed a militarily significant quantity of chemical weapons, and there were widespread fears in the United States and elsewhere that terrorists might gain control of some of this arsenal. The concern was sufficiently great that the Western countries were willing to work with the Assad regime, previously considered a pariah, in order to dispose of these weapons.[79] Significantly, the dangers could have included a nuclear dimension, given Syria's abortive effort to build nuclear infrastructure, terminated in 2007 when Israel destroyed a nuclear reactor about to become operational. As one former U.S. government official notes, "Think of how much more dangerous to the entire region the Syrian civil war would be today if Assad had a nuclear reactor, and even perhaps nuclear weapons, in hand."[80] There are certainly other countries on the list of potential proliferators that might raise similar concerns.[81]

---

77. White House Press Office, "Remarks by President Barack Obama, Hradcany Square, Prague, Czech Republic, April 5, 2009," April 5, 2009, available from *www.whitehouse.gov/the_press_office/Remarks-By-President-Barack-Obama-In-Prague-As-Delivered.*

78. *National Security Strategy of the United States* (Washington, D.C.: The White House, 2006).

79. Patrick J. McDonnell, "Push to Eliminate Syria's Chemical Weapons May Extend Assad's Rule," *Los Angeles Times*, October 15, 2013, available from *articles.latimes.com/2013/oct/15/world/la-fg-syria-assad-20131015.*

80. Elliott Abrams, "Bombing the Syrian Reactor: The Untold Story," *Commentary* 135, No. 2 (February 2013): 24; and Bruce Riedel, "Lessons of the Syrian Reactor," National Interest, No. 125, May 2013, 39–46, expresses similar views.

81. Certainly, it is likely that many in Washington would have concerns should Saudi Arabia decide to pursue a nuclear weapon, as some senior Saudi officials have intimated. While the Saudi kingdom has been remarkably stable, it also was the home of Osama bin Laden and has been an important recruiting ground for al Qaida and other Salafist terrorist groups. On Saudi nuclear ambitions, see

In his original writings, Waltz argued that unstable states were "un-likely to initiate nuclear projects," but in any case discounted the concern because he doubted nuclear weapons would be employed during internal strife. He did not address the dangers of nuclear terrorism (nor did he address the risk that loss of control might result in nuclear proliferation if another country gained access to weapons).[82] Waltz addressed the problem in his more recent writings, but dismissed the concerns as either overblown or not made worse by the spread of nuclear weapons to more countries.[83] He did not address the problem of failed states at all.

In this sense, Waltz had a far more simplistic view of the terrorism problem than either those who worry about it or even those who are more dismissive. He is far more complacent than others sometimes identified as "proliferation optimists." For example, Bueno de Mes-quita, another so-called "proliferation optimist," saw terrorism as a significant risk associated with additional nuclear proliferation.[84]

The Complexity of Crisis Management

For U.S. policymakers, a nuclear crisis between third parties is a nightmare scenario. It is easy to assert that nuclear deterrence is in-herently stable. It is more difficult to demonstrate in practice. U.S. policymakers knew, either from personal experience or from stud-

---

Brandon Friedman, "Alternatives to U.S. Hard Power: The Saudi Response to U.S. Tactics in the Middle East," *Foreign Policy Research Institute E-Notes*, accessed January 27, 2014, available from *www.fpri.org/articles/2014/01/alter-natives-us-hard-power-saudi-response-us-tactics-middle-east*; and Mark Urban, "Saudi Nuclear Weapons 'On Order' from Pakistan," *BBC News*, November 6, 2013, available from *www.bbc.co.uk/news/world-middle-east-24823846*.

82. Waltz, *The Spread of Nuclear Weapons: More May Be Better*, 12.

83. The book has appeared in several editions, originally in Sagan and Waltz, *The Spread of Nuclear Weapons: A Debate Renewed: With New Sections on In-dia and Pakistan, Terrorism, and Missile Defense*, 126–130.

84. Bueno de Mesquita and Riker, 304.

ies of nuclear history, that managing nuclear crises with the Soviet Union were fraught with danger. While many came to trust in the experience and wisdom of their colleagues and Soviet adversaries, they also realized that there was a learning curve. No one comes born into the world understanding the manifest complexities of policymaking in the context of a nuclear crisis. Hence, it is perhaps not surprising that U.S. policymakers have worried about the dangers confronting the world as policymakers in other countries climb the learning curve of nuclear strategy.[85]

Why should policymakers in Washington care about what happens elsewhere, especially when the U.S. national interest may not be at risk? One reason is that in the era of globalization, the United States has interests in most countries vulnerable to the negative consequences of a nuclear war. A nuclear exchange between India and Pakistan, for example, could lead to tens of millions of deaths, potentially including many U.S. citizens, even if one does not accept recent theories about the prospects for climatic impacts induced by a regional war involving tens of nuclear weapons.[86] Such a conflict also would cause negative economic and political repercussions, including some specifically related to the role of nuclear weapons in international relations, such as potentially undermining

---

85. Michael Horowitz, "The Spread of Nuclear Weapons and International Conflict: Does Experience Matter?," *Journal of Conflict Resolution* 53, No. 2 (April 2009): 234–257, argues that new nuclear weapons states are "significantly more likely to reciprocate militarized challenges and have their challenges reciprocated," compared with states that have possessed the weapons for longer periods of time.

86. Some policymakers are likely to take seriously the environmental risks of a regional nuclear conflict, while others may discount the concern, given their views on climate change. There is now a small literature claiming that there will be global environmental impacts. Owen B. Toon et al., "Consequences of Regional-Scale Nuclear Conflicts," *Science* 315, No. 5816 (March 2007): 1224–1225; O. B. Toon, et al., "Atmospheric Effects and Societal Consequences of Regional Scale Nuclear Conflicts and Acts of Individual Nuclear Terrorism," *Atmospheric Chemistry and Physics* 7, No. 8 (April 2007): 1973–2002; and A. Robock, et al., "Climatic Consequences of Regional Nuclear Conflicts," *Atmospheric Chemistry and Physics* 7, No. 8 (April 2007): 2003–2012.

the taboo against operational employment of nuclear weapons.[87]

Hence, it is not surprising that U.S. policymakers moved into high gear when there was a threat that a conflict between India and Pakistan had the potential to escalate. While such crises have been rare, there were two of them in a short period of time during the Clinton and George W. Bush administrations.

In many ways, this is an intensely personal concern for policymakers. There were two occasions, 1999 and 2001-2002, during which U.S. policymakers worried that a war might erupt between the two countries. The 1999 Kargil crisis started when Pakistan infiltrated forces into parts of Kashmir that the Indians thought belonged to them and thereby threatened Indian lines of supply. The Indians attacked the Pakistani positions, and, when it proved impossible to overcome the Pakistanis in the difficult mountain terrain, escalated the conflict by launching air strikes. All of this occurred under a nuclear shadow, the two countries having tested nuclear weapons the year before.[88]

U.S. policymakers clearly took this crisis seriously, and viewed it in a nuclear context from the very beginning. After all, the consequences of a nuclear exchange were frightening. Estimates put the death toll from an attack on Bombay at between 150,000 and 850,000.[89] It is thus not surprising that U.S. President Bill Clinton

---

87. For a discussion of the range of impacts on U.S. interests resulting from a nuclear exchange between India and Pakistan, based on a wargame played at the Naval War College in 1999, see Paul D. Taylor, "India and Pakistan," Naval War College Review, Vol. 54, No. 3, Summer 2001, 40–51.

88. Neil Joeck, "The Indo-Pakistani Nuclear Confrontation: Lessons from the Past, Contingencies for the Future," in Henry D. Sokolski, ed., *Pakistan's Nuclear Future: Reining in the Risk* (Carlisle, PA: Strategic Studies Institute, 2009), 19–23, available from *www.npolicy.org/books/Pakistan_Nuclear_Future/Ch1_Joeck.pdf.*

89. Bruce Riedel, *American Diplomacy and the 1999 Kargil Summit at Blair House* (Philadelphia: Center for the Advanced Study of India, University of Pennsylvania, 2002), 3–4.

took a personal role in trying to convince the Pakistanis to with-draw from the territory that they had occupied, and that diplomacy involved the most senior officials in the United States government with responsibility for South Asian affairs, including from both the military and State Department.[90]

The same level of involvement emerged at the time of the 2001-2002 Twin Peaks crisis. In December 2001, terrorists subsequently linked to the Pakistani intelligence services attacked the Indian Parliament. The Indians responded by mobilizing their military and prepared to mount retaliatory attacks, leading the Pakistanis to mobilize their own military. The following May, terrorists at-tacked Indian military encampments near the border between the two countries, killing both soldiers and family members.[91]

On-going military operations in Afghanistan in the wake of our intervention following the 9/11 attacks by al Qaeda made these events even more worrying to U.S. policymakers. In essence, a war between India and Pakistan, not to mention a nuclear exchange, would put at risk the U.S. military forces operating in Afghanistan. As happened in the previous crisis, the diplomacy involved senior level U.S. government officials, and reflected the same degree of concern as the earlier crisis.

---

90. The intensity of the engagement is reflected in one statistic offered by Strobe Talbott, Deputy Secretary of State: between 1998 (after the Indian nuclear test) and the end of 2000, he met 14 times with his Indian counterpart. See, Strobe Talbott, *Engaging India: Diplomacy, Democracy, and the Bomb* (Washington, DC: Brookings Institution Press, 2004), 3–4. At the time of the Kargil crisis, the diplomacy also involved the Commander, U.S. Central Command, and other State Department and National Security Council officials in addition to President Clinton and Talbott, according to Riedel, *American Diplomacy and the 1999 Kargil Summit at Blair House*, 4–5.

91. Joeck, "The Indo-Pakistani Nuclear Confrontation: Lessons from the Past, Contingencies for the Future," 29–31; and Moeed Yusuf, "U.S. as Interlocu-tor in Nuclear Crises: Deriving Future Policy Implications from a Study of the 2001-2002 India-Pakistan Standoff," in *A Collection of Papers from the 2009 Nuclear Scholars Initiative* (Washington, DC: Center for Strategic and Interna-tional Studies, 2009), 49–50.

Thus, even in a situation where the United States had no intention of providing extended deterrence, nuclear weapons created a complex problem for international diplomacy. Indeed, some argue that one of the intended roles for Pakistan's nuclear arsenal was to force U.S. diplomatic interventions in crises with India.[92]

An Argument for All Persuasions

The arguments supporting pessimism about the consequences of nuclear proliferation cover such a wide range of issues that almost any U.S. policymaker can find one sufficiently compelling to guide his or her actions. A Democratic advocate of nuclear zero and a Republican opponent of the Comprehensive Nuclear-Test-Ban Treaty can find common ground in the arena of nuclear nonproliferation, even if the arguments that they find most compelling differ fundamentally.[93] Such policymakers, while convinced that nuclear deterrence works and perhaps even believing that nuclear weapons make the world unsafe for the prosecution of large scale conventional wars, also tend to believe that the workings of nuclear deterrence are potentially problematic and certainly have no faith that its sometimes Byzantine logic will work in every situation.

This is not to say that all policymakers are devotees of nonproliferation; quite the contrary. Many policymakers found and find nonproliferation efforts in tension with other policies, and it is often evident that those other policies take precedence. Policymakers tend towards proliferation relativism, viewing the problem in a

---

92. Yusuf, 47; and Narang, 49–50; S. P. Kapur, "Ten Years of Instability in a Nuclear South Asia," *International Security* 33, No. 2 (Fall 2008): 76, doi:10.1162/isec.2008.33.2.71.

93. Evident from the agreement shown in Congressional Commission on the Strategic Posture of the United States, *America's Strategic Posture: The Final Report of the Congressional Commission on the Strategic Posture of the United States.*

broader context that takes account of other issues as well.[94]

Yet, to find nonproliferation an obstacle to other policy objectives is rather different from arguing its reverse. Most officials who tolerated or condoned specific instances of nuclear proliferation apparently did not do so because they thought the spread of nuclear weapons was a positive thing but because they believed the available policy alternatives were even worse. While perhaps not provable, it seems clear that no senior U.S. government official ever actively promoted nuclear proliferation as a general principle, although admittedly some did on occasion actively support proliferation in specific cases.

In this sense, Waltz has done the field a profound disservice, because a whole debate has been defined by his writings. His views are widely cited in the academic literature to present the case for nuclear optimism, even though his arguments are more appropriately referred to as proliferation optimism. Waltz offers a straw man that presents grossly simplified versions of the complex and rich strategic thinking that has characterized the practice of nuclear strategy. While Sagan and other critics appropriately take Waltz to task, they are less concerned about the practice of nuclear strategy then they are about highlighting the very real risks from nuclear proliferation. The result is that the perspectives of those who have conceptualized, developed, or implemented nuclear policy, strategy, and operations are lost, and academic students refer to Waltz as though his work represents the depths of the subject.

In contrast to the rich complexity and nuance of writings on U.S. nuclear strategy, which take into account the vagaries of the world confronting national leaders, Waltz offered a simple, straightforward assessment. While John Gaddis views nuclear weapons as one of many factors accounting for the "long peace," Waltz fixated on their role. While two generations of nuclear policymakers worried about the limitations of nuclear deterrence, articulated since

94. Lavoy, "The Strategic Consequences of Nuclear Proliferation: A Review Essay," 753.

the mid-1950s in theories of limited war, Waltz adopted an absolutist position that makes former Secretary of State John Foster Dulles and the doctrine of Massive Retaliation appear subtle by comparison.

U.S. policymakers have a range of reasons for seeing Waltz's arguments as irrelevant to the world they face.[95] For them, Panglossian world views are no substitute for the potentially deadly realities of armed strife in the real world. Ultimately, the academic debate between proliferation optimists and pessimists is exactly that, academic. Thus, it is not surprising that few, if any, officials responsible for national security responsibilities will find the perspectives of the proliferation optimists attractive, while many will work actively to prevent proliferation. The only surprising thing is that some people seem to think that there is something to debate.[96]

---

95. The reaction of some former and current policymakers shown this chapter is perhaps telling. They found the discussion of "more is better" so totally irrelevant to their own experience and world view that they could not understand why anyone would waste their time looking at the subject. Many have read Waltz, only to dismiss his work as an intellectual curiosity, perhaps interesting as a pedagogic tool but not of value for someone engaged in shaping the world.

96. Academic students of international relations worry about perceived and real disconnects between their efforts to develop theory and the activity of practitioners. See Stephen M. Walt, "The Relationship Between Theory and Policy in International Relations," Annual Review of Political Science, Vol. 8, No. 1, June, 2005: 23–48. Unfortunately, the work of nuclear proliferation optimists and the debate between academic optimists and pessimists only confirms the suspicion of policymakers that there is little to be learned from those trying to build credible theory.

CHAPTER 3

At All Costs:
The Destructive Consequences of
Antiproliferation Policy

John Mueller

Over the decades, analysts of nuclear proliferation have separated themselves, or have been separated by others, into two camps.[1]

Proliferation alarmists constitute the vast majority, occupying a prominent position in what Bernard Brodie once called "the cult of the ominous."[2] They argue that proliferation is a dire development that must be halted as a supreme policy priority. Thus, Graham Allison argues that "no new nuclear weapons states" should be a prime foreign policy principle, and Joseph Cirincione insists that nonproliferation should be "our number one national-security priority."[3] Of late such alarmism has been sent into high relief by the apparent efforts of Iran to move toward a nuclear bomb capacity. In the presidential campaign of 2008, candidate Barack Obama repeatedly announced that he would "do everything in [his] power

---

1. Scott D. Sagan and Kenneth N. Waltz, *The Spread of Nuclear Weapons: A Debate Renewed, Second Edition* (New York: Norton, 2002).

2. Bernard Brodie, *Escalation and the Nuclear Option* (Princeton, NJ: Princeton University Press, 1966), 93.

3. Graham Allison, *Nuclear Terrorism: The Ultimate Preventable Catastrophe* (New York: Times Books, 2004), Ch. 7; and Joseph Cirincione, "Cassandra's Conundrum," *National Interest,* No. 92, (November–December 2007): 15.

to prevent Iran from obtaining a nuclear weapon—everything," while candidate John McCain insisted that Iran must be kept from obtaining a nuclear weapon "at all costs."[4] Neither bothered to tally what "everything" might entail and what the costs might be, and both continue to make the same kinds of pronouncements.

The other camp, which is quite tiny, consists of proliferation sanguinists who maintain that, on balance, a certain amount of proliferation might actually enhance international stability by deterring war or warlike adventures.[5]

However, there is another possible approach to the proliferation issue that might be called irrelevantist. People in this near-empty camp stress two considerations:

First, it really doesn't bloody well *matter* whether the bomb proliferates or not: proliferation has been of little consequence (except on agonies, obsessions, rhetoric, posturing, and spending), and no country that has possessed the weapons has found them useful or beneficial, nor have those who abandoned them suffered loss because of this. Thus, the consequences of such proliferation that has taken place have been substantially benign: those who have acquired the weapons have "used" them simply to stoke their egos or to deter real or imagined threats.

Second, alarmed efforts to prevent the proliferation of nuclear weapons have proved to be very costly, leading to the deaths of more people than perished at Hiroshima and Nagasaki combined.

---

4.   Barack Obama, Remarks at the American Israel Public Affairs Committee's Annual Policy Conference, Washington, DC, June 4, 2008, available   from   *www.nytimes.com/2008/06/04/us/politics/04text-obama-aipac. html?pagewanted=all&_r=0*; and Tim Reid and Tom Baldwin, "Nuclear Iran Must Be Stopped at All Costs, Says McCain," *Times* (London), January 26, 2006.

5. For example, Kenneth Waltz, "Why Iran Should Get the Bomb: Nuclear Balancing Would Mean More Stability," *Foreign Affairs* 91, No. 4 (July/August 2012), available from *www.foreignaffairs.com/articles/137731/kenneth-n-waltz/ why-iran-should-get-the-bomb*.

This chapter evaluates these two irrelevantist considerations.[6]

The Benign Consequences of Proliferation

Although we have now suffered through two-thirds of a century characterized by alarmism about the disasters inherent in nuclear proliferation, the substantive consequences of proliferation have been quite limited.

Military Value

Although the weapons have certainly generated obsession and have greatly affected military spending, diplomatic posturing, and ingenious theorizing, the few countries to which the weapons have proliferated have for the most part found them a notable waste of time, money, effort, and scientific talent. They have quietly kept them in storage and haven't even found much benefit in rattling them from time to time.

There has never been a militarily compelling—or even minimally sensible—reason to use nuclear weapons, particularly because of an inability to identify suitable targets or ones that could not be attacked as effectively by conventional munitions. And it is difficult to see how nuclear weapons benefited their possessors in specific military ventures. Israel's presumed nuclear weapons did not restrain the Arabs from attacking in 1973, nor did Britain's prevent Argentina's seizure of the Falklands in 1982. Similarly, the tens of thousands of nuclear weapons in the arsenals of the enveloping allied forces did not cause Saddam Hussein to order his occupying forces out of Kuwait in 1990. Nor did possession of the bomb benefit America in Korea, Vietnam, Iraq, or Afghanistan; France in

---

6. This chapter draws on ideas and approaches presented in John Mueller, *Atomic Obsession: Nuclear Alarmism from Hiroshima to al-Qaeda* (New York: Oxford University Press, 2010).

Algeria; or the Soviet Union in Afghanistan.[7]

Domination

Proliferation alarmists may occasionally grant that countries principally obtain a nuclear arsenal to counter real or perceived threats,
but many go on to argue that the newly nuclear country will then
use its nuclear weapons to "dominate" the area. That argument was
repeatedly used with dramatic urgency before 2003 for the dangers
supposedly posed by Saddam Hussein, and it has also been frequently applied to Iran.

Exactly how that domination business is to be carried out is never
made clear.[8] But the notion, apparently, is that should an atomic
Iraq (in earlier fantasies) or North Korea or Iran (in present ones)
rattle the occasional rocket, other countries in the area, suitably
intimidated, would supinely bow to its demands. Far more likely,
any threatened states will make common cause with each other and
with other concerned countries against the threatening neighbor.
It seems overwhelmingly likely that if a nuclear Iran brandishes
its weapons to intimidate others or to get its way, it will find that
those threatened, rather than capitulating to its blandishments or
rushing off to build a compensating arsenal of their own, will ally
with others to stand up to the intimidation—rather in the way they
coalesced into an alliance of convenience to oppose Iraq's invasion
of Kuwait in 1990.

It is also argued that nuclear weapons embolden a country to do
mischief with less fear of punishing consequences. However, coun-

---

7. For an extended discussion, see Mueller, Atomic Obsession, especially Chap-
ters 4 and 5.

8. On this issue, see in particular Stephen M. Walt, "Containing Rogues and
Renegades: Coalition Strategies and Counterproliferation," in Victor A. Utgoff,
ed., *The Coming Crisis: Nuclear Proliferation, U.S. Interests, and World Order*
(Cambridge, MA: MIT Press, 2000), 191–226.

tries like Iran already seem about as free as they need to be to do mischief (from the U.S. standpoint) in the Middle East and rogue states like the USSR, China, and North Korea do not seem to have stepped up their mischief after gaining nuclear weapons.

Deterrence

Although there are conceivable conditions under which nuclear weapons could serve a deterrent function, it is questionable whether they have yet ever done so. In particular, it is far from clear that nuclear weapons are what kept the Cold War from becoming a hot one.

The people who have been in charge of world affairs since World War II have been the same people or the intellectual heirs of the people who tried assiduously, frantically, desperately, and, as it turned out, pathetically, to prevent World War II, and when, despite their best efforts, world war was forced upon them, they found the experience to be incredibly horrible, just as they had anticipated. On the face of it, to expect these countries somehow to allow themselves to tumble into anything resembling a repetition of that experience—whether embellished with nuclear weapons or not—seems almost bizarre. The people running world politics since 1945 have had plenty of disagreements, but they have not been so obtuse, depraved, flaky, or desperate as to need visions of mushroom clouds to conclude that another world war, nuclear or non-nuclear, win or lose, could be decidedly unpleasant.[9]

Moreover, each leak from the archives suggests that the Soviet Union never seriously considered any sort of direct military aggression against the United States or Europe. Thus, Robert Jervis: "The Soviet archives have yet to reveal any serious plans for unprovoked aggression against Western Europe, not to mention a first

---

9. John Mueller, *Quiet Cataclysm* (New York: HarperCollins, 1995), Ch. 5; and Idem, *Atomic Obsession*, Ch. 3.

strike against the United States." Vojtech Mastny: "The strategy of nuclear deterrence [was] irrelevant to deterring a major war that the enemy did not wish to launch in the first place....All Warsaw Pact scenarios presumed a war started by NATO." Stephen Ambrose: "At no time did the Red Army contemplate, much less plan for, an offensive against West Europe." According to Bernard Brodie, "It is difficult to discover what meaningful incentives the Russians might have for attempting to conquer Western Europe." And George Kennan: "I have never believed that they have seen it as in their interests to overrun Western Europe militarily, or that they would have launched an attack on that region generally even if the so-called nuclear deterrent had not existed."[10]

As Kennan suggests, given the Soviets' global game plan, which stressed revolutionary upheaval and subversion from within, not Hitlerian conquest, and given their experience with two disastrous world wars, another such experience scarcely made any sense whatever. That is, there was nothing to deter.

Status Symbols

Moreover, the weapons have not proved to be crucial status—or virility—symbols. French President Charles de Gaulle did opine in 1965 that "no country without an atom bomb could properly consider itself independent," and Robert Gilpin concluded that "the possession of nuclear weapons largely determines a nation's rank

---

10 . Robert Jervis, "Was the Cold War a Security Dilemma?" *Journal of Cold War Studies* 3, No. 1 (Winter 2001): 59; Vojtech Mastny, "Introduction," in Vojtech Mastny, Sven G. Holtsmark, and Andreas Wenger, eds., War Plans and Alliances in the Cold War: Threat Perceptions in the East and West, London and New York: Routledge, 2006, 3; Stephen E. Ambrose, "Secrets of the Cold War," New York Times, December 27, 1990; Bernard Brodie, Escalation and the Nuclear Option, 71–72; George F. Kennan, "Containment Then and Now," Foreign Affairs, Vol. 65, No. 4, Spring 1987, 888-889; and also Robert H. Johnson, Improbable Dangers: U.S. Conceptions of Threat in the Cold War and After, New York: St. Martins, 1994, 29.

in the hierarchy of international prestige."[11] In Gilpinian tradition, some analysts who describe themselves as "realists" have insisted for years that Germany and Japan must soon come to their senses and quest after nuclear weapons.[12]

As Jervis has observed however, "India, China, and Israel may have decreased the chance of direct attack by developing nuclear weapons, but it is hard to argue that they have increased their general prestige or influence."[13] And, as Jenifer Mackby and Walter Slocombe note:

> Undoubtedly some countries have pursued nuclear weapons more for status than for security. However, Germany, like its erstwhile Axis ally, Japan, has become powerful because of its economic might rather than its military might, and its renunciation of nuclear weapons may even have reinforced its prestige. It has even managed to achieve its principal international objective—reunification—without becoming a nuclear state.[14]

---

11. Charles de Gaulle, "The Thoughts of Charles de Gaulle," *New York Times Magazine*, May 12, 1968, 103; and Robert Gilpin, *War and Change in World Politics* (New York: Cambridge University Press, 1981), 215.

12. Christopher Layne contended in 1993 that Japan by natural impulse must soon come to yearn for nuclear weapons. Christopher Layne, "The Unipolar Illusion: Why New Great Powers Will Rise," *International Security* 17, No. 4 (Spring 1993): 5–51. And three years earlier, John Mearsheimer argued that "Germany will feel insecure without nuclear weapons." John Mearsheimer, "Back to the Future: Instability in Europe after the Cold War," *International Security* 15, No. 1 (Summer 1990): 5–56.

13. Robert Jervis, *The Meaning of the Nuclear Revolution* (Ithaca, NY: Cornell University Press, 1989), 4. For an assessment of this issue, see Jacques E.C. Hymans, *The Psychology of Nuclear Proliferation: Identity, Emotions, and Foreign Policy* (New York: Cambridge University Press, 2006), 211 212.

14. Jennifer Mackby and Walter Slocombe, "Germany: A Model Case, A Historical Imperative," in Kurt M. Campbell, Robert J. Einhorn, and Mitchell B. Reiss, eds., *The Nuclear Tipping Point: Why States Reconsider Their Nuclear*

How much more status would Japan have if it possessed nuclear weapons? Would anybody pay a great deal more attention to Britain or France if their arsenals held 5,000 nuclear weapons, or would anybody pay much less if they had none? Did China need nuclear weapons to impress the world with its economic growth? Or with its Olympics?

Pace of Proliferation

These considerations help explain why alarmists have been wrong for decades about the pace of nuclear proliferation. Dozens of technologically capable countries have considered obtaining nuclear arsenals, but very few have done so. Indeed, as Jacques Hymans has pointed out, even supposedly optimistic forecasts about nuclear dispersion have proved to be too pessimistic.[15] Thus, in 1958 the National Planning Association predicted "a rapid rise in the number of atomic powers ... by the mid-1960s."[16] A few years later C. P. Snow sternly predicted, "Within, at the most, six years, China and several other states [will] have a stock of nuclear bombs" while U.S. President John Kennedy observed that there might be "ten, fifteen, twenty" countries with a nuclear capacity by 1964.[17]

Choices (Washington, DC: Brookings Institution Press, 2004), 210.

15. Hymans, *The Psychology of Nuclear Proliferation*, 5.

16. NPA Special Project Committee on Security through Arms Control, *1970 without Arms Control*, Planning Pamphlet No. 104 (Washington, DC: National Planning Association, 1958), 42.

17. C.P. Snow, "The Moral Un-Neutrality of Science," *Science* 133, No. 3448, (January 27, 1961), 259; and John F. Kennedy in Sidney Kraus, ed., *The Great Debates: Kennedy vs. Nixon, 1960* (Bloomington: University of Indiana Press, 1962) 394. Kennedy reportedly considered a Chinese nuclear test "likely to be historically the most significant and worst event of the 1960s." William Burr and Jeffrey T. Richelson, "Whether to 'Strangle the Baby in the Cradle'," *International Security* 25, No. 3 (Winter 2000-01), 61. Actually, that designation should probably go instead to Kennedy's decision to send American troops in substantial numbers to Vietnam largely to confront the Chinese "threat" that was

Such punditry has gone astray in part because the pundits insist on extrapolating from the wrong cases. A more pertinent proto-type would have been Canada, a country that could easily have had nuclear weapons by the 1960s but declined to make the effort.[18] In fact, over the decades, a huge number of countries capable of developing nuclear weapons have neglected even to consider the opportunity—for example, Canada, Italy, and Norway—even as Argentina, Brazil, Libya, South Korea, and Taiwan have backed away from or reversed nuclear weapons programs, and Belarus, Kazakhstan, South Africa, and Ukraine have actually surrendered or dismantled an existing nuclear arsenal.[19] Some of that reduction is no doubt due to the hostility of the nuclear nations, but even without that the Canadian case seems to have proved to have rather general relevance. Its experience certainly suggests, as Stephen Meyer has shown, there is no "technological imperative" for coun-tries to obtain nuclear weapons once they have achieved the techni-cal capacity to do so.[20]

---

deemed to lurk there.

18. For a discussion of the relevance of the Canadian case, concluding from it that the issue of nuclear proliferation—then often known as the "Nth country problem"—was approaching "a finite solution," see John Mueller, "Incentives for Restraint: Canada as a Nonnuclear Power," *Orbis* 11, No. 3 (Fall 1967): 864–884. For some early commentary suggesting that alarm about nuclear prolifera-tion was unjustified, see Richard N. Rosecrance, "International Stability and Nuclear Diffusion," in Richard N. Rosecrance, ed., T*he Dispersion of Nuclear Weapons: Strategy and Politics* (New York: Columbia University Press, 1964), 293–314.

19. William M. Arkin, "The Continuing Misuses of Fear," *Bulletin of the Atomic Scientists* 62, No. 5 (September–October 2006), 45; Mitchell Reiss, *Bridled Am-bition: Why Countries Constrain Their Nuclear Capabilities* (Washington, DC: Woodrow Wilson Center Press), 1995; and T.V. Paul, *Power versus Prudence: Why Nations Forgo Nuclear Weapons* (Montreal: McGill–Queen's University Press, 2000).

20. Stephen M. Meyer, *The Dynamics of Nuclear Proliferation* (Chicago: Uni-versity of Chicago, 1984); see also Hymans, *Psychology of Nuclear Prolifera-tion*, 2-12. On the very limited impact of the Nuclear Nonproliferation Treaty, see Mueller, *Atomic Obsession*, Ch. 9.

In consequence, alarmist predictions about proliferation chains, cascades, dominoes, waves, avalanches, epidemics, and points of no return have proved to be faulty. Insofar as most leaders of most countries (even rogue ones) have considered acquiring the weapons, they have come to appreciate several defects: nuclear weapons are dangerous, distasteful, costly, and likely to rile the neighbors. Moreover, as Hymans has demonstrated, the weapons have also been exceedingly difficult to obtain for administratively dysfunctional countries like Iran.[21]

Potential Dangers

Even if nuclear weapons so far have had little impact, there is an array of potential (or imagined) dangers that, alarmed antiproliferators suggest, might come about.

Crazy Leaders

It is sometimes said, or implied, that proliferation has had little consequence because the only countries to possess nuclear weapons have had rational leaders. But nuclear weapons have proliferated to large, important countries run by unchallenged monsters who, at the time they acquired the bombs, were certifiably deranged: Josef Stalin, who in 1949 was planning to change the climate of the Soviet Union by planting a lot of trees, and Mao Zedong, who in 1964 had just carried out a bizarre social experiment that resulted in an artificial famine in which tens of millions of Chinese perished.[22]

---

21. Jacques E.C. Hymans, *Achieving Nuclear Ambitions: Scientists, Politicians, and Proliferation* (New York: Cambridge University Press, 2012); and Idem, "Crying Wolf about an Iranian Nuclear Bomb," *Bulletin of the Atomic Scientists,* January 17, 2012, available from *thebulletin.org/crying-wolf-about-iranian-nuclear-bomb.*

22. On Stalin's mental condition, see John Mueller, R*etreat from Doomsday: The Obsolescence of Major War* (New York; Free Press, 1989), 123; On Mao,

It is incumbent on those who strongly oppose an Iranian bomb to demonstrate that the Iranian regime is daffier than these.

Atomic Terrorism

Thus far, terrorist groups seem to have exhibited only limited desire and even less progress in going atomic. That lack of action may be because, after a brief exploration of the possible routes, they—unlike generations of alarmists—have discovered that the tremendous effort required is scarcely likely to be successful.[23]

In the wake of 9/11, however, concern about the atomic terrorist surged even though the attacks of that day used no special weapons. By 2003, United Nations Ambassador John Negroponte judged there to be "a high probability" that within two years al-Qaeda would attempt an attack using a nuclear weapon or other weapon of mass destruction. In that spirit Graham Allison published a book in 2004—over ten years ago—relaying his "considered judgment" that "on the current path, a nuclear terrorist attack on America in the decade ahead is more likely than not."[24] Allison has quite a bit of company in his unfulfilled alarmist conclusions. According to Robert Gates, former secretary of defense, every senior government leader is kept awake at night by "the thought of a terrorist

---

see Frank Dikötter, *Mao's Great Famine: The History of China's Most Devastating Catastrophe, 1958–1962* (New York: Walker, 2010).

23. For an extended discussion, see Mueller, *Atomic Obsession*, Ch. 12–15.

24. John D. Negroponte, "Letter Dated 17 April 2003 from the Permanent Representative of the United States of America to the United Nations addressed to the chairman of the Committee," United Nations Security Council, document S/AC.37/2003/(1455)/26, April 22, 2003, available from *www.globalsecurity. org/security/library/report/2003/n0335167.pdf*; and Allison, *Nuclear Terrorism*, 15. He had presumably relied on the same inspirational mechanism in 1995 to predict that "in the absence of a determined program of action, we have every reason to anticipate acts of nuclear terrorism against American targets before this decade is out." Idem, "Must We Wait for the Nuclear Morning After?" *The Washington Post*, April 30, 1995.

ending up with a weapon of mass destruction, especially nuclear."[25] And in 2010, President Barack Obama held the atomic terrorist to be "the single biggest threat to U.S. security."[26]

One route a would-be atomic terrorist might take would be to receive or buy a bomb from a generous, like-minded nuclear state for delivery abroad. That route is highly improbable, however, because there would be too much risk—even for a country led by extremists—that the ultimate source of the weapon would be discovered. As one prominent analyst, Matthew Bunn, puts it, "A dictator or oligarch bent on maintaining power is highly unlikely to take the immense risk of transferring such a devastating capability to terrorists they cannot control, given the ever-present possibility that the material would be traced back to its origin."[27] Important in this last consideration are deterrent safeguards afforded by "nuclear forensics," which is the rapidly developing science (and art) of connecting nuclear materials to their sources even after a bomb has been exploded.[28]

Moreover, there is a very considerable danger to the donor that the bomb (and its source) would be discovered before delivery or that it would be exploded in a manner and on a target the donor would

25. Quoted in, Bob Graham, Chairman, *World at Risk: The Report of the Commission on the Prevention of WMD Proliferation and Terrorism* (New York: Vintage, 2008), 43.

26. White House Press Office, "Remarks by President Obama and President Zuma of South Africa before Bilateral Meeting," Blair House, Washington, DC, April 11, 2010, available from *www.whitehouse.gov/the-press-office/remarks-president-obama-and-president-zuma-south-africa-bilateral-meeting.*

27. Matthew Bunn, *Securing the Bomb 2007* (Cambridge, MA, and Washington, DC: Project on Managing the Atom, Harvard University, and Nuclear Threat Initiative, 2007), vi; see also William Langewiesche, *The Atomic Bazaar* (New York: Farrar, Straus and Giroux, 2007), 20; and Brian Michael Jenkins, *Will Terrorists Go Nuclear?* (Amherst, NY: Prometheus, 2008), 198.

28. For an excellent discussion of nuclear forensics, see Michael A. Levi, *On Nuclear Terrorism* (Cambridge MA: Harvard University Press, 2007), 127–133.

not approve of—including on the donor itself. Another concern would be that the terrorist group might be infiltrated by foreign intelligence.[29]

In addition, almost no one would trust al-Qaeda. As one observer has pointed out, the terrorist group's explicit enemies list includes not only Christians and Jews but also all Middle Eastern regimes; Muslims who don't share its views; most Western countries; the governments of Afghanistan, India, Pakistan, and Russia; most news organizations; the United Nations; and international nongovernmental organizations.[30] Most of the time, al-Qaeda didn't get along all that well even with its host in Afghanistan, the Taliban government.[31]

There has also been great worry about "loose nukes," especially in post-communist Russia—weapons, "suitcase bombs" in particular, that can be stolen or bought illicitly. A careful assessment conducted by the Center for Nonproliferation Studies has concluded that it is unlikely that any of those devices have been lost and that, regardless, their effectiveness would be very low or even nonexistent because they (like all nuclear weapons) require continual maintenance.[32] Even some of those people most alarmed by the prospect of atomic terrorism have concluded, "It is probably true that there are no 'loose nukes,' transportable nuclear weapons missing from their proper storage locations and available for purchase in some

---

29. Robin M. Frost, *Nuclear Terrorism after 9/11* (London: International Institute for Strategic Studies, 2005), 64; Jenkins, 143; and Keir A. Lieber and Daryl G. Press, "Why States Won't Give Nuclear Weapons to Terrorists," *International Security* 38, No. 1, (Summer 2013), 80-104.

30. Peter Bergen, "Where You Bin? The Return of Al Qaeda," *New Republic*, January 29, 2007, 19.

31. Lawrence Wright, The Looming Tower: Al-Qaeda and the Road to 9/11 (New York: Knopf, 2006), 230–231, 287–288.

32. Center for Nonproliferation Studies, *"Suitcase Nukes": A Reassessment* (Monterey, CA: Monterey Institute of International Studies, 2002), 4, 12; Langewiesche, 19; and Jenkins, 149–150.

way."[33]

It might be added that Russia has an intense interest in controlling any weapons on its territory because it is likely to be a prime target of any illicit use by terrorist groups, particularly Chechen ones with whom it has been waging a vicious on-and-off war for decades. The government of Pakistan, which has been repeatedly threatened by terrorists, has a similar interest in controlling its nuclear weapons and material—and scientists. As noted by Stephen Younger, former head of nuclear weapons research and development at Los Alamos National Laboratory, "Regardless of what is reported in the news, all nuclear nations take the security of their weapons very seriously."[34] Even if a finished bomb were somehow lifted somewhere, the loss would soon be noted and a worldwide pursuit launched.

Moreover, finished bombs are outfitted with devices designed to trigger a non-nuclear explosion that would destroy the bomb if it were tampered with. And there are other security techniques: Bombs can be kept disassembled with the components stored in separate high-security vaults, and security can be organized so that two people and multiple codes are required not only to use the bomb but also to store, maintain, and deploy it. If the terrorists seek to enlist (or force) the services of someone who already knows how to set off the bomb, they would find, as Younger stresses, that "only few people in the world have the knowledge to cause an unauthorized detonation of a nuclear weapon." Weapons designers know how a weapon works, he explains, but not the multiple types of signals necessary to set it off, and maintenance personnel are trained in only a limited set of functions.[35]

---

33. Anna M. Pluta and Peter D. Zimmerman, "Nuclear Terrorism: A Disheartening Dissent," *Survival* 48, No. 2 (Summer 2006), 56; and Stephen M. Younger, *The Bomb: A New History* (New York: Ecco Press, 2009), 152.

34. Stephen M. Younger, *Endangered Species* (New York: Ecco Press, 2007), 93; and Younger, *The Bomb*, 152–153.

35. Ibid., 153–54. On triggers, see Jenkins, 141. On disassembled parts, see

There could be dangers in the chaos that would emerge if a nuclear state were to fail, collapsing in full disarray—Pakistan is frequently brought up in this context and sometimes North Korea as well. However, even under those conditions, nuclear weapons would likely remain under heavy guard by people who know that a purloined bomb would most likely end up going off in their own territory; would still have locks (and in the case of Pakistan would be disassembled); and could probably be followed, located, and hunted down by an alarmed international community. The worst-case scenario in that instance requires not only a failed state but also a considerable series of additional permissive conditions, including consistent (and perfect) insider complicity and a sequence of hasty, opportunistic decisions or developments that click flawlessly in a manner far more familiar to Hollywood scriptwriters than to people experienced with reality.[36]

Accidental or Inadvertent Detonation

A common concern has been that the weapons would somehow go off, by accident or miscalculation, devastating the planet in the process. In 1960, a top nuclear strategist declared it "most unlikely" that the world could live with an uncontrolled arms race for decades.[37] And in 1979, political scientist Hans J. Morgenthau declared: "The world is moving ineluctably towards a third world war—a strategic nuclear war. I do not believe that anything can be done to prevent it. The international system is simply too un-

---

Reiss, 11 and 13; and Joby Warrick, "Pakistan Nuclear Security Questioned," *Washington Post*, November 11, 2007.

36. For a discussion of the failed-state scenario, including useful suggestions for making it even less likely, see Levi, 133–138. On the unlikelihood of a Pakistan collapse, see Juan Cole, "Obama's Domino Theory," *Salon*, March 30, 2009, available from *www.salon.com/2009/03/30/afghanistan_7*.

37. Herman Kahn, *On Thermonuclear War* (Princeton, NJ: Princeton University Press, 1960), x.

stable to survive for long."[38] And Eric Schlosser remains deeply concerned about that danger today.[39]

In a 1982 New Yorker essay and best-selling book, both titled The Fate of the Earth, Jonathan Schell passionately, if repetitively, argued the not entirely novel proposition that nuclear war would be terrible, and he concluded ominously: "One day—and it is hard to believe that it will not be soon—we will make our choice. Either we will sink into the final coma and end it all or, as I trust and believe, we will awaken to the truth of our peril... and rise up to cleanse the earth of nuclear weapons."[40]

As it happened, both options were avoided: Neither final coma nor nuclear cleansing ever took place. The common alarmist prognostications assuming that because the weapons exist, sooner or later one or more of them will necessarily go off has now failed to deliver for 70 years, and this suggests that something more than luck is operating.

The Costly Consequences of Antiproliferation Policies

Although the consequences of nuclear proliferation have proved to be substantially benign, the same cannot be said for the consequences of the nuclear antiproliferation quest. The perpetual agony over nuclear proliferation has resulted in an obsessive effort to prevent or channel it, and it is this effort, not proliferation itself, that has inflicted severe costs.

---

38. Quoted, Francis Anthony Boyle, World Politics and International Law (Durham, NC: Duke University Press, 1985), 73; and Marc Trachtenberg, The Cold War and After: History, Theory, and the Logic of International Politics (Princeton, NJ: Princeton University Press, 2012), 25.

39. Eric Schlosser, Command and Control (New York: Allen Lane/Penguin Books, 2013). For commentary, see John Mueller, "Fire, Fire," Times Literary Supplement, March 7, 2014, 26.

40. Jonathan Schell, The Fate of the Earth (New York: Knopf, 1982), 231.

The Costs in Iraq

The war in Iraq, with deaths that have run well over a hundred thousand (and counting)—greater than those inflicted at Hiroshima and Nagasaki combined—is a key case in point.[41] It is far from clear, however, what Saddam Hussein, presiding over a deeply resentful population and an unreliable army (fearing overthrow, he was wary about issuing his army bullets and would not allow it within 30 miles of Baghdad with heavy equipment), could have done with a tiny number of bombs against his neighbors and their massively armed well-wishers other than seek to stoke his ego and to deter real or imagined threats. He was, then, fully containable and deterrable.[42] The war against him was a militarized antiproliferation effort substantially sold as a venture required to keep his pathetic regime from developing nuclear and other presumably threatening weapons and to prevent him from palming off some of these to eager and congenial terrorists.[43] The notion that the war was designed to spread democracy in the Middle East did gain significance but, as Bruce Russett notes, only after the antiproliferation arguments for going to war proved to be empty; or, as Francis Fukuyama has put it, a prewar request to spend "several hundred billion dollars

---

41. For both, estimates start at around 110,000 with many ranging higher, see "Casualties of the Iraq War," *Wikipedia*, last modified March 12, 2015, available from *en.wikipedia.org/wiki/Casualties_of_the_Iraq_War*; and "The Atomic Bombings of Hiroshima and Nagasaki: Total Casualties," Atomic Archive, available from *www.atomicarchive.com/Docs/MED/med_chp10.shtml*.

42. See Mueller, *Atomic Obsession*, 133. For ammunition, see James Fallows, "Why Iraq Has No Army," *Atlantic*, December 2005, 72. For heavy weapons, see Maggie O'Kane, "Saddam Wields Terror—and Feigns Respect," *Guardian*, November 24, 1998. For critical pre-war examinations of the assumption that Iraq, however armed, posed much of a threat, see John J. Mearsheimer and Stephen M. Walt, "Iraq: An Unnecessary War," *Foreign Policy* 82, No. 1, (January/February 2003), 50–59; Brink Lindsay and John Mueller, "Should We Invade Iraq?" *Reason*, January 2003; and John Mueller, *Overblown* (New York: Free Press, 2006), 131–133.

43. Olivier Roy, "Europe Won't Be Fooled Again," *New York Times*, May 13, 2003.

and several thousand American lives in order to bring democracy to . . . Iraq" would "have been laughed out of court."[44]

Thus, in an influential 2002 book, Kenneth Pollack strenuously advocated a war whose "whole point" would be to "prevent Saddam from acquiring nuclear weapons," which Western intelligence agencies, he reported, were predicting would occur by 2004 (pessimistic) or 2008 (optimistic).[45] He fully recognized the costs of the war he advocated, costs that he felt might cause thousands of deaths and run into the tens of billions of dollars. But war would be worth this price, concluded Pollack, because with nuclear weapons Saddam would become the "hegemon" in the area, allowing him to control global oil supplies.[46] The nuclear theme was repeatedly applied by the administration in the run-up to the war, most famously, perhaps, in National Security Adviser Condoleezza Rice's dire warning about waiting to have firm evidence before launching a war: "We don't want the smoking gun to be a mushroom cloud." As the Defense Department's Paul Wolfowitz pointed out, nuclear weapons, or at any rate weapons of mass destruction (WMDs), were the "core reason" used for selling the war.[47] At a press briefing on April 10, 2003, shortly after the fall of Baghdad, White House

---

44. Bruce Russett, "Bushwhacking the Democratic Peace," *International Studies Perspectives* 6, No. 4 (November 2005): 396; Francis Fukuyama, "America's Parties and Their Foreign Policy Masquerade," *Financial Times*, March 8, 2005; John Mueller, *War and Ideas: Selected Essays* (London and New York: Routledge, 2011), Ch. 7; and Jon Western, Selling Intervention and War: The Presidency, The Media, and Public Opinion, Baltimore and London: Johns Hopkins University Press, 2005, Ch. 6.

45. Kenneth M. Pollack, *The Threatening Storm: The Case for Invading Iraq* (New York: Random House, 2003), 418.

46. Ibid., xiv, 335, 413, 418. Pollack also estimated that another $5 to $10 billion over the first three years would be required for rebuilding (p. 397).

47. Sam Tannenhaus, "Interview with Paul Wolfowitz," *Vanity Fair*, May 9, 2003; and "Wolfowitz: WMD Chosen as Reason for Iraq War for 'Bureaucratic Reasons,'" *CNN.com*, May 30, 2003, available from *transcripts.cnn.com/TRANSCRIPTS/0305/30/se.08.html*.

press secretary Ari Fleischer insisted, "We have high confidence that they have weapons of mass destruction. That is what this war was about and it is about." And Karl Rove, one of Bush's top political advisers, reflected in 2008 that, absent the belief that Saddam Hussein possessed WMD, "I suspect that the administration's course of action would have been to work to find more creative ways to constrain him like in the 90s."[48]

For their part, Democrats have derided the war as "unnecessary," but the bulk of them only came to that conclusion after the United States was unable to find either nuclear weapons or weapons programs in Iraq. Many of them have made it clear they would support putatively preemptive (actually, preventive) military action and its attendant bloodshed if the intelligence about Saddam's programs had been accurate.[49]

However, the devastation of Iraq in the service of limiting proliferation did not begin with the war in 2003. For the previous 13 years, that country had suffered under economic sanctions visited upon it by both Democratic and Republican administrations that were designed to force Saddam from office (and, effectively, from life since he had no viable sanctuary elsewhere) and to keep the country from developing weapons, particularly nuclear ones. Multiple, although disputed, studies have concluded that the sanctions were the necessary cause of hundreds of thousands of deaths in the country, most of them children under the age of five—the most innocent of civilians.[50]

---

48. Sam Stein, "Rove: We Wouldn't Have Invaded Iraq If We Knew the Truth about WMDs," *Huffington Post*, December 2, 2008, available from *www.huffingtonpost.com/2008/12/02/rove-we-wouldnt-have-inva_n_147923.html*. Some still consider it "open to debate," however, "that the war was fought primarily as a nonproliferation campaign." Henry D. Sokolski, *Underestimated: Our Not So Peaceful Nuclear Future* (Arlington, VA: Nonproliferation Policy Education Center, 2015),4 note 7.

49. On this issue, see also Arkin, 45.

50. Richard Garfield, *Morbidity and Mortality Among Iraqi Children from 1990*

The Costs in North Korea

The costly alarmist perspective on atomic proliferation is also evident in policies advocated toward North Korea at various times. Thus, proposed Graham Allison in 2004, if diplomacy failed, a Pearl Harbor like attack should be launched even though potential targets had been dispersed and disguised and even though a resulting war might kill tens of thousands in the South.[51]

Members of the Bush administration, perhaps because they had become immersed in their own anti proliferation war in Iraq at the time, were able to contain their enthusiasm for accepting Allison's urgent advice, and North Korea has since become something of a nuclear weapons state. In 2004 Allison had sternly insisted that such an outcome would be "gross negligence" and would foster "a transformation in the international security order no great power would wittingly accept." We are now in position, then, to see if his confident predictions have come true: A North Korean bomb, he declared, would "unleash a proliferation chain reaction, with South Korea and Japan building their own weapons by the end of the decade" (that is by 2009), with Taiwan "seriously considering following suit despite the fact that this would risk war with China," and with North Korea potentially "becoming the Nukes R Us for

to 1998 (South Bend, IN: Kroc Institute for International Peace Studies, University of Notre Dame, 1999); John Mueller and Karl Mueller, "The Methodology of Mass Destruction: Assessing Threats in the New World Order," *Journal of Strategic Studies* 23, No. 1 (March 2000), 163, 187; Matt Welch, "The Politics of Dead Children," *Reason*, (March 2002): 53-58; Pollack, 138 and 139; Mohamed M. Ali, John Blacker, and Gareth Jones, "Annual mortality rates and excess deaths of children under five in Iraq, 1991-1998," *Population Studies* 57, No. 2 (2003): 217-226; and Andrew Cockburn and Patrick Cockburn, *Out of the Ashes: The Resurrection of Saddam Hussein* (New York: HarperCollins, 1999), Ch. 5. However, for the argument, based on later intelligence, that high estimates of a half-million or more child deaths are likely exaggerated due in particular to regime manipulation of the numbers, see Michael Spagat, "Truth and death in Iraq under sanctions," *Significance* 7, No. 3 (September 2010), 116-120.

51. Allison, *Nuclear Terrorism*, 165 and 171.

terrorists."[52]

The same mentality was shown by decisionmakers in the Clinton administration in 1994. The United States never actually sent troops into action in its confrontation with North Korea at that time, but it certainly edged threateningly in that direction when a U.S. National Intelligence Estimate concluded that there was "a better than even" chance that North Korea had the makings of a small nuclear bomb. This conclusion was hotly contested by other American analysts and was later "reassessed" by intelligence agencies and found possibly to have been overstated. In addition, even if North Korea had the "makings" in 1994, skeptics pointed out, it still had several key hurdles to overcome in order to develop a deliverable weapon.[53]

Nonetheless, the Clinton administration was apparently prepared to go to war with the miserable North Korean regime to prevent or to halt its nuclear development.[54] Accordingly, it moved to impose deep economic sanctions to make the isolated country even poorer (insofar as that was possible), a measure which garnered no support even from neighboring Russia, China, and Japan.[55] It also moved to engage in a major military buildup in the area. So apocalyptic (or simply paranoid) was the North Korean regime about these two developments that some important figures think it might have gone to war on a preemptive basis if the measures had been carried out.[56] A full scale war on the peninsula, estimated the

---

52. Ibid., 166.

53. Don Oberdorfer, *The Two Koreas: A Contemporary History* (New York: Basic Books, 2001), 307-308, 316; Selig S. Harrison, *Korean Endgame: A Strategy for Reunification and U.S. Disengagement* (Princeton, NJ: Princeton University Press, 2002), 213; and James Fallows, "The Panic Gap: Reactions to North Korea's Bomb," *National Interest*, No. 38 (Winter 1994/95): 40-45.

54. Oberdorfer, 308, 316.

55. Ibid., 318.

56. Ibid., 329; and Derek D. Smith, *Deterring America: Rogue States and the*

Pentagon, not perhaps without its own sense of apocalypse, could kill 1,000,000 people including 80,000 to 100,000 Americans, cost over $100 billion, and do economic destruction on the order of a trillion dollars.[57] A considerable price, one might think, to prevent a pathetic regime from developing weapons with the potential for killing a few tens of thousands—if they were actually exploded, an act that would surely be suicidal for the regime.

In the next years, floods and bad weather exacerbated the economic disaster that had been inflicted upon the country by its rulers. Famines ensued, and the number of people who perished reached hundreds of thousands or more, with some careful estimates putting the number at over two million.[58] Although food aid was eventually sent from the West, there seem to have been systematic efforts in the early days of the famine in particular to deny its existence for fear that a politics free response to a humanitarian disaster would undercut efforts to use food aid to wring diplomatic concessions on the nuclear issue from North Korea.[59]

Encouraging Extortion

Due to its antiproliferation fixation, the United States has often allowed itself to become a victim of extortion. North Korea has undoubtedly been the greatest winner in this somewhat tricky process when the regime accepted a $4 billion energy package for its cooperation in 1994.[60] But Taiwan and South Korea have also es-

Proliferation of Weapons of Mass Destruction (Cambridge, UK: Cambridge University Press, 2006),70, 71.

57. Oberdorfer, 324; and Harrison, 117, 118.

58. Oberdorfer, 399; and Andrew S. Natsios, The Great North Korean Famine (Washington, DC: *United States Institute of Peace Press*, 2001), 215.

59. Ibid., 147, 148.

60. Reiss, 327.

sentially extorted funds from the hand-wringers by accepting funds and favors and then giving in to what is likely to be their own best interests. Israel played the game in a different way during its 1973 war. After being attacked by Egypt and Syria, Israel made it known that it might use its nuclear weapons in the conflict (it may have had 20 at the time), a move that reportedly forced the United States desperately to initiate an immediate and massive resupply of the Israel military, aiding in Israel's subsequent victory against the invading Arab armies.[61]

The American reputation generated by this episode for being a willing victim of extortion also had the perverse result of fueling, or supplying a rationale for, South Africa's nuclear ambitions. As one South African official put it, "We argued that if we cannot use a nuclear weapon on the battlefield (as this would have been suicidal), then the only possible way to use it would be to leverage intervention from the Western Powers by threatening to use it. We thought that this might work and the alleged Israel-USA case gave some support to our view."[62]

Hampering Economic Development

Leonard Weiss notes that "restrictions on nuclear trade and development are important elements of a nonproliferation regime."[63]

---

61. There was also a strong perception in Israel that the United States might like to see the Arabs win some ground, something that might help compel Israel to negotiate a peace treaty later. The result of Israel's atomic gambit seems to have undercut support for that approach to the degree that it existed. On these issues, see Seymour M. Hersh, *The Samson Option: Israel's Nuclear Arsenal and American Foreign Policy* (New York: Random House, 1991), 40, 139, 226–39; and T.V. Paul, *The Tradition of Non-Use of Nuclear Weapons* (Stanford, CA: Stanford University Press, 2009), 127–128.

62. Peter Liberman, "The Rise and Fall of the South African Bomb," *International Security* 26, No. 2 (Fall 2001): 62; and Reiss, 15, 28.

63. Leonard Weiss, "Safeguards and the NPT: Early History Portended Current

Antiproliferation efforts can thus hamper worldwide economic development by increasing the effective costs of developing nuclear energy. As countries grow, they require ever increasing amounts of power. Any measure that limits their ability to acquire this vital commodity—or increases its price—effectively slows economic growth at least to some degree and thereby reduces the gains in life expectancy inevitably afforded by economic development.

In the various proclamations about controlling the proliferation of nuclear weapons, this cost goes almost entirely unconsidered. For example, one of the common proposals by antiproliferators is that no country anywhere (except those already doing it) should be able to construct any facilities that could produce enriched uranium or plutonium—substances that can be used either in advanced reactors or in bombs. The Nuclear Nonproliferation Treaty (NPT) does specifically guarantee to signing non-nuclear countries "the fullest possible exchange of technology" for the development of peaceful nuclear power. However, as Richard Betts points out, this guarantee has been undermined by the development of a "nuclear suppliers cartel" that has worked to "cut off trade in technology for reprocessing plutonium or enriching uranium," thereby reducing the NPT to "a simple demand to the nuclear weapons have-nots to remain so." Under some proposals, the cartel would be extended to fuel as well.[64]

Antiproliferator Allison is among those advocating the cartelization of nuclear fuel. He further suggests that nuclear states guarantee to sell the non-nuclear ones all the nuclear fuel they need (presumably in perpetuity) at less than half price, but does not attempt

---

Problems," in Henry Sokolski, ed., *Nuclear Nonproliferation Treaty Missteps* (Carlisle, PA: Strategic Studies Institute, forthcoming).

64. Richard K. Betts, "Universal Deterrence or Conceptual Collapse? Liberal Pessimism and Utopian Realism," in Victor A. Utgoff , ed., *The Coming Crisis: Nuclear Proliferation, U.S. Interests, and World Order* (Cambridge, MA, MIT Press, 2000), 70.

to calculate the price tag for this.[65] The 2008 Graham Commission, of which Allison was a member, repeats this demand, though it suggests that nuclear fuel be made available at market prices "to the extent possible." It, too, eschews cost considerations.[66] There is, however, a glimmer of evidence that the economic cost of hampering the nuclear industry has been considered at least in passing by some dedicated antiproliferators. In a 2007 plea that the world be made free of nuclear weapons, four former top policy officials insisted that the use of highly enriched uranium be phased out from civil commerce and that it be removed from all the research facilities in the entire world, a costly demand that was not repeated in their 2008 version.[67]

The antiproliferation obsession has also resulted in the summary dismissal of potentially promising ideas for producing energy. Thomas Schelling points out that there was a proposal in the 1970s (a decade that experienced two major shocks in the price of oil) to safely explode tiny thermonuclear bombs in underground caverns to generate steam to produce energy in an ecologically clean manner. According to Schelling, the proposal was universally rejected by both arms control and energy policy analysts at the time "without argument, as if the objections were too obvious to require articulation."[68] On closer exploration, of course, this scheme might have proved unfeasible for technical or economic reasons. But to dismiss it without any sort of analysis was to blithely sacrifice en-

---

65. Allison, *Nuclear Terrorism*, 156–165.

66. Graham, *World at Risk*, xx.

67. George P. Shultz, William J. Perry, Henry A. Kissinger, and Sam Nunn, "A World Free of Nuclear Weapons," *Wall Street Journal*, January 4, 2007; and George P. Shultz, William J. Perry, Henry A. Kissinger, and Sam Nunn, "Toward a Nuclear-Free World," *Wall Street Journal*, January 15, 2008.

68. Thomas C. Schelling, "An Astonishing Sixty Years: The Legacy of Hiroshima," Nobel Prize Lecture, Stockholm, Sweden, December 8, 2005, 369, available from *nobelprize.org/nobel_prizes/economics/laureates/2005/schelling-lecture.html*.

ergy needs—and therefore human welfare—to antiproliferation knee-jerk.

Something similar may now be in the cards. Currently in the research phase, it may become possible in the future to reduce radically the cost of producing nuclear energy by using lasers for isotope separation to produce the fuel required by reactors.[69] This, of course, might also make it easier, or at any rate less costly, for unpleasant states to develop nuclear weapons. Accordingly, a balanced assessment of costs and benefits would have to be made if the technique ever proves to be feasible. But there is an excellent chance no one will ever make it: like the technology Schelling discusses, it will be dismissed out of hand. Relatedly, the antiproliferation obsession has also sometimes hampered the potentially valuable expansion of nuclear power to ships, particularly to icebreakers.

Enhancing Dependence on Foreign Oil

There is also something of a security aspect to this process. Ever since the oil shocks of the 1970s, it has become common in American politics to espy a danger to the country's security in allowing it to be so dependent on a product that is so disproportionately supplied to the world by regimes in the Middle East that are sometimes contemptible, hostile, and/or unstable. One obvious solution would be to rely much more on nuclear energy. There are a number of reasons why this has failed to happen, but the association of nuclear power with nuclear weapons and with worries about nuclear proliferation have had the result of making it much more difficult and expensive—often prohibitively so—to build nuclear reactors.[70]

---

69. Mark Anderson, "Beware New Nukes," *Wired*, October 2008, 182.

70. On this issue, see especially Spencer R. Weart, *Nuclear Fear: A History of Images* (Cambridge, MA: Harvard University Press, 1988).

Undercutting Efforts to Prevent Global Warming

In addition, because nuclear power does not emit greenhouse gases, it is an obvious potential candidate for helping with the problem of global warming, an issue many people hold to be of the highest concern for the future of the planet. Since many of the policies arising from the nonproliferation fixation increase the costs of nuclear power, they, to that degree, exacerbate the problem.

Exacerbating the Nuclear Waste Problem

The antiproliferation focus has also exacerbated the nuclear waste problem in the United States. In the late 1970s, the Carter administration banned the reprocessing (or recycling) of nuclear fuel, something that radically reduces the amount of nuclear waste, under the highly questionable assumption that this policy would reduce the danger of nuclear proliferation.[71]

Encouraging Proliferation

Moreover, antiproliferation efforts can be counterproductive in their own terms. As Mitchell Reiss observes, "one of the unintended 'demonstration' effects" of the American antiproliferation war against Iraq "was that chemical and biological weapons proved insufficient to deter America: only nuclear weapons, it appeared, could do this job."[72] It is likely a lesson North Korea has drawn.

---

71. Richard L. Garwin and Georges Charpak, *Megawatts and Megatons: A Turning Point in the Nuclear Age?* (New York: Knopf, 2001), 144–145.

72. Mitchell B. Reiss, "The Nuclear Tipping Point: Prospects for a World of Many Nuclear Weapons States," in Kurt M. Campbell, Robert J. Einhorn, and Mitchell B. Reiss, eds., *The Nuclear Tipping Point: Why States Reconsider Their Nuclear Choices* (Washington, DC: Brookings Institution Press, 2004), 12.

Israel: The Potential for Self-Destruction

I am not a fan of worst case scenarios. However, one that may be worthy of consideration concerns the danger that, stoked by an obsession over atomic weapons in the hands of Iran, Israel could essentially destroy itself—that is, cease to exist as a coherent Jewish state—without a single Iranian bomb ever being developed.[73]

There have been extreme apprehensions in Israel about atomic annihilation at the hands of Iran, and these have sometimes inspired a sense of despair and desperation—and in many quarters a loss of hope.[74] Indeed, Yossi Klein Halevi and Michael Oren observed in early 2007 that "military men suddenly sound like theologians when explaining the Iranian threat." And some of the ponderings were downright spooky:

> Ahmadinejad's pronouncements about the imminent return of the Hidden Imam and the imminent destruction of Israel aren't regarded as merely calculated for domestic consumption; they are seen as glimpses into an apocalyptic game plan. Ahmadinejad has reportedly told his Cabinet that the Hidden Imam will reappear in 2009—precisely the date when Israel estimates Iran will go nuclear.[75]

The existential danger for Israel in this arises not so much from Iran's capacity or potential capacity to do harm—though judicious and balanced concerns about that danger are, of course, justified—as from the consequences of the hype, at once apoplectic and apoc-

---

73. See also John Mueller and Ian S. Lustick, "Israel's Fight-or-Flight Response," *National Interest*, No. 98 (November/December 2008): 68-71.

74. Benny Morris, "Israel's unhappy birthday," *Los Angeles Times*, May 11, 2008; and Ian S. Lustick, "Abandoning the Iron Wall: Israel and 'the Middle Eastern Muck'," *Middle East Policy* XV, No. 3, (August 2008).

75. Yossi Klein Halevi and Michael B. Oren, "Israel's Worst Nightmare," *New Republic*, January 30, 2007. For later, but similar, apocalyptic visions, see Ari Shavit, "The Bomb and the Bomber," *New York Times*, March 21, 2012.

alyptic, over the prospective Iranian bomb. The problem is that, if the hysteria persists, a considerable and increasing number of Israelis may be led to conclude that since there is no way to guarantee that Iran will never be able to obtain a bomb, the situation is hopeless, that Israel is ultimately doomed, and that it is best to live elsewhere—in a place where one can bring up children free from nuclear fears.

"There is nothing more regular in Jewish history and myth than Jews 'returning' to the Land of Israel to build a collective life," observed Ian Lustick in 2008, "except for Jews leaving the country and abandoning the project." And "so far, in the twenty first century," he continued, "more Jews have left than have arrived," noting a survey indicating that only 69 percent of Jewish Israelis say they want to stay in the country.[76] He also cites a 2007 poll indicating that one quarter of Israelis were considering leaving the country, including almost half of all young people.[77] Jeffrey Goldberg points to another survey finding that 44 percent of Israelis say they are ready to leave if they could find a better standard of living elsewhere and notes that "the emigration of Israel's most talented citizens is a constant worry of Israeli leaders."[78]

Thus, there is some danger that wallowing in its atomic obsession, Israel will scare itself into extinction.

Bombing Iran

Barack Obama's administration is notable for the apparent absence of anyone (else) in a high foreign policy office who clearly and publicly opposed the war on Iraq before George W. Bush launched

---

76. "Israel's Future: The Time Factor," A Debate between Efraim Inbar and Ian S. Lustick, *Israel Studies Forum* 23, No. 1, (Summer 2008): 6, 10.

77. Lustick, "Abandoning the Iron Wall."

78. Jeffrey Goldberg, "Unforgiven," *Atlantic*, May 2008, 40.

his invasion.[79] However, due in considerable part to the subsequent disastrous experience in that enterprise—a disaster that continues to evolve and unfold—misgivings about the wisdom and consequences of launching a Pearl Harbor-like military strike on Iran's nuclear facilities increased over time.

Among the considerations:

• Following from the previous discussion, if the rattled and insecure Iranian leadership was lying when it repeatedly proclaims it had no intention of developing nuclear weapons or if it were to undergo a conversion from that position (triggered perhaps by an Israeli airstrike), it would likely soon find, like all other nuclear-armed states, that the bombs are essentially useless and a very considerable waste of time, effort, money, and scientific talent.

• If Iran were to seek to develop nuclear weapons, the process, contrary to intelligence exaggerations persistently spun out, would likely take years or even decades. For example, it was in March 2010 that Doyle McManus conveyed the information that "most experts now estimate that Iran needs about 18 months to complete a nuclear device and a missile to carry it," although it needed to overcome "technical bottlenecks, the exposure of secret facilities and equipment breakdowns."[80] Hymans, unlike the "experts" McManus consulted, goes much deeper, stressing the administrative difficulties of developing a bomb. These require "the full-hearted cooperation of thousands of scientific and technical workers for many years." The task is "enormous," and

> the key driver of an efficient nuclear weapons project has not been a country's funding levels, politi-

---

79. John Mueller, "What Americans Get That the Foreign Policy Elite Doesn't," *Huffington Post*, May 30, 2014, available from *www.huffingtonpost.com/john-mueller/what-americans-get-that-t_b_5420173.html*.

80. Doyle McManus, "What if Iran gets the bomb? Many now argue that containment, not a military strike, is the best way to deal with Tehran's nuclear ambitions," *Los Angeles Times*, March 21, 2010.

cal will, or access to hardware. Rather, the key has been managerial competence. Nuclear weapons projects require a hands-off, facilitative management approach, one that permits scientific and technical professionals to exercise their vocation. But states such as Iran tend to feature a highly invasive, authoritarian management approach that smothers scientific and technical professionalism. Thus, it is very likely that Iran's political leadership—with its strong tendency toward invasive, authoritarian mismanagement—has been its own worst enemy in its quest for the bomb.[81]

• Iran scarcely has a viable delivery system for nuclear weapons.[82]

• If Iran were to develop nuclear weapons, it would most likely "use" them in the same way all other nuclear states have: for prestige (or ego-stoking) and to deter real or perceived threats.[83] Indeed, as Thomas Schelling suggests, deterrence is about the only value the weapons might have for Iran. Such devices, he points out, "would be too precious to give away or to sell" and "too precious to waste killing people" when they could make other countries "hesitant to consider military action."[84] Actually, in the wake of the Iraq disaster, Iran has scarcely needed nuclear weapons for deterrence.

---

81. Hymans, "Crying wolf about an Iranian nuclear bomb." See also Idem, *Achieving Nuclear Ambitions*.

82. Richard L. Garwin, "Evaluating Iran's missile threat," *Bulletin of the Atomic Scientists* 64, No. 2 (May/June 2008): 40; and "Pentagon Appears to Downgrade Iran Strategic Missile Threat," *Global Security Newswire*, July 11, 2014, available from *www.nti.org/gsn/article/pentagon-appears-downgrade-iran-icbm-threat-assessment/*.

83. For the conclusion that these would be Iran's sole motivations, see Colin Dueck and Ray Takeyh, "Iran's Nuclear Challenge," *Political Science Quarterly* 122 (Summer 2007): 195.

84. Schelling.

It can credibly deter an invasion by the Americans simply by maintaining a trained and well-armed cadre of a few thousand troops dedicated to, and capable of, inflicting endless irregular warfare on the invaders.

• The leadership of Iran, however hostile and unpleasant in many ways, does not consist of a self-perpetuating gaggle of suicidal lunatics. Thus, as Schelling suggests, it is exceedingly unlikely Iran would give nuclear weapons to a substate group like Hezbollah to detonate—particularly on a country like Israel—not least because the non-lunatics in charge would fear that the source of the weapon would be detected by nuclear forensics inviting devastating retaliation.

• An Iranian bomb would be unlikely to trigger a cascade of proliferation in the Middle East. Although Joseph Cirincione has held that a nuclear Iran could readily be deterred from using a nuclear weapon against its neighbors or the United States, and although he discounts the likelihood that it might "intentionally give a weapon to a terrorist group they could not control," he has set off on an extravagant alarmist fear cascade envisioning "a nuclear chain reaction where states feel they must match each other's nuclear capability." This, he concludes, "could lead to a Middle East with not one nuclear weapons state, Israel, but four or five," and that "is a recipe for nuclear war."[85] However, as noted earlier, if Iran were to brandish nuclear weapons, it would find itself, like Iraq in 1990, confronting a coalition of convenience made up of countries far stronger militarily.

---

85. Cirincione, 16, 17. Cirincione has much company. As Potter and Mukhatzhanova observe, "Today it is hard to find an analyst or commentator on nuclear proliferation who is not pessimistic about the future. It is nearly as difficult to find one who predicts the future without reference to metaphors such as proliferation chains, cascades, dominoes, waves, avalanches, and tipping points." However, after considerable study and research on the issue, they finally became "convinced that the metaphor is inappropriate and misleading, as it implies a process of nuclear decisionmaking and a pace of nuclear weapons spread that are unlikely to transpire." William C. Potter and Gaukhar Mukhatzhanova, "Divining Nuclear Intentions," *International Security* 33, No. 1 (Summer 2008): 159.

• The long term negative consequences for Israel from an attack on Iranian nuclear facilities either by Israel or by the United States could surpass those that developed even from such ill advised ventures as Israel's 1982 invasion of Lebanon and its government-induced policy to encourage settlement in occupied territories. And the casualties inflicted by an attack on Iran by direct action and by its "collateral damage" (including, potentially, induced nuclear radiation) could conceivably be considerable. Moreover, the results would most likely be counterproductive. Israel's highly touted air strike against Iraq's nuclear program in the Osirak attack of 1981, as Dan Reiter and Richard Betts have pointed out, actually caused Saddam Hussein to speed up his nuclear program 25-fold while decreasing its vulnerability by dispersing its elements—a lesson Iran has also learned.[86]

• In the end, it is incumbent upon those who have advocated a Pearl Harbor-like attack on Iran to demonstrate that the rather innocuous history of nuclear proliferation over the last two-thirds of a century is irrelevant and that the regime there is daffier and more threatening than, for example, the ultimate rogue, China, in 1964.[87]

Conclusion

In 1950, notes John Lewis Gaddis, no one among foreign policy decisionmakers anticipated most of the major international developments that were to take place in the next half-century. Among

---

86. Dan Reiter, "Preventive Attacks against Nuclear Programs and the 'Success' at Osiraq," *Nonproliferation Review* 12, No. 2 (July 2005): 355-371; Ibid., *Preventive War and Its Alternatives: The Lessons of History* (Carlisle, PA: Strategic Studies Institute, U.S. Army War College, 2006), 4, 6; and Richard K. Betts, "The Osirak Fallacy," *National Interest*, No. 83 (Spring 2006): 22-25. Moreover, as Hymans also stresses in Achieving Nuclear Ambitions, the reactor the Israelis bombed was not even capable of producing weapons-grade fissile material.

87. See Francis J. Gavin, "Blasts from the Past: Proliferation Lessons from the 1960s," *International Security* 29, No. 3 (Winter 2004/05): 100–135.

these were "that there would be no World War" and that the United States and the USSR, "soon to have tens of thousands of thermonuclear weapons pointed at one another, would agree tacitly never to use any of them."[88]

However, as discussed earlier, it could have been reasonably argued at the time that major war was simply not in the cards—that despite the huge differences on many issues, the leading countries of the world would manage to keep themselves from plunging into a self-destructive cataclysm like, or even worse than, the one they had just survived. This perspective was not, of course, the only one possible, but there was no definitive way to dismiss it. Thus, as a matter of simple, plain, rational decision making, this prospect—the one that proved to be true—should have been on the table.

If no one anticipated this distinct possibility in 1950, the irreverent might be led ungraciously to suggest that the United States would have been better served if those at the summit of foreign policy had been replaced by coin-flipping chimpanzees who would at least occasionally get it right from time to time out of sheer luck. (The chimps would have to flip coins because the animals are all too human and would likely otherwise fall into patterns of repetitive, and probably agitated, behavior.)

We seem to be at it again. Just about the whole of the foreign policy establishment has taken it as a central article of faith that the proliferation of nuclear weapons is an overwhelming danger and that all possible measures, including war, must be taken to keep it from happening.[89]

---

88. John Lewis Gaddis, *George F. Kennan: An American Life* (New York: Penguin, 2011), 403.

89. Thus, it is impressive how casually the sanguinist perspective of Kenneth Waltz—a plausible line of argument, whatever my reservations—has been commonly dismissed without even much analysis or effort at refutation. As Richard Betts notes, the argument cannot simply be "brushed off," yet that is exactly what has happened; "surprisingly few academic strategists" have tried to refute it in detail. Betts, "Universal Deterrence or Conceptual Collapse?" 64. Thus the

Concern is justified I suppose, but the experience of two-thirds of a century suggests that any danger is far from overwhelming. It would certainly be preferable that a number of regimes never obtain nuclear weapons. Indeed, if the efforts to dissuade Iran from launching a nuclear weapons program succeed, they would be doing it a favor—though, quite possibly, the Iranians won't notice.

The handful of countries that have acquired nuclear weapons seem to have done so sometimes as an ego trip for current leaders, and more urgently (or perhaps merely in addition) as an effort to deter a (supposed) potential attack on themselves: China to deter the United States and the Soviet Union, Israel to deter various enemy nations in the neighborhood, India to deter China, Pakistan to deter India, and now North Korea to deter the United States and maybe others.[90] Insofar as nuclear proliferation is a response to perceived threat, it follows that one way to reduce the likelihood such countries would go nuclear is a simple one: stop threatening them.

More generally, any antiproliferation priority should be topped

---

generally careful and thoughtful Mitchell Reiss worries (or did in 2004) that we are nearing a nuclear "tipping point" that could trigger a "proliferation epidemic." Should this occur, he assures us, "few would take comfort in the assurances of some academic theorists [a double putdown if there ever was one] that 'more may be better,'" directly quoting Waltz, but not even affording him a footnote. Reiss, "The Nuclear Tipping Point," 4. If academics have substantially ignored the argument, policymakers have been at least as oblivious. For example, James Kurth simply dismisses the Waltz argument out of hand: "There probably has not been a single foreign policy professional in the U.S. government," he noted in 1998, "that has found this notion to be helpful." James Kurth, "Inside the Cave: The Banality of I.R. Studies," *National Interest*, No. 53 (Fall 1998). But not, one strongly suspects, because any has spent any time thinking about it.

90. On China, see Mueller, *Atomic Obsession*, 144. Hymans puts prime emphasis on ego—with the added proviso that only when the ego in charge has a conception of a national identity that can be considered to be what he calls "of the oppositional nationalist" variety will the country really try to get nuclear weapons. Hymans, *Psychology of Nuclear Proliferation*. For somewhat related findings, see Etel Solingen, *Nuclear Logics* (Princeton, NJ: Princeton University Press, 2007). See also the discussion in Potter and Mukhatzhanova.

with a somewhat higher one: avoiding militarily aggressive actions under the obsessive sway of worst-case-scenario fantasies, actions that might lead to the deaths of tens—or hundreds—of thousands of people.[91]

"It is dangerous," muses Hymans aptly, "to fight smoke with fire."[92] Nuclear proliferation, while not particularly desirable, is unlikely to accelerate or prove to be a major danger, and extreme antiproliferation policies need careful reconsideration. They can generate costs far higher than those likely to be inflicted by the potential (and often essentially imaginary) problems they seek to address.

---

91. The phrase "worst case fantasies" is from Bernard Brodie, "The Development of Nuclear Strategy," *International Security* 2, No. 4 (Spring 1978): 68.

92. Hymans, *Psychology of Nuclear Proliferation*, 225.

CHAPTER 4

Should We Let it All Go?

Victor Gilinsky

The traditional criticism of U.S. efforts to stop the spread of the bomb has been that we can't do much about it. (Decades ago former U.S. Defense Secretary Harold Brown quipped that he could replace all the government's nonproliferation experts and diplomats with two—one to announce each additional nuclear state, and the other to wring his hands over the increase.) But no one questioned the bomb's importance. John Mueller takes a different tack; he says the whole thing doesn't matter. My assignment is to take issue with the broad thesis of his chapter, "At All Costs: The Destructive Consequences of Antiproliferation Policy."[1] He questions the significance, past and future, of the spread of nuclear weapons, and whether there is ever a compelling case for their use. He questions even more the efforts to restrain the spread: He concludes that antiproliferation efforts have proved exceedingly costly, and—counting in this category the 2003 Iraq invasion—have led to more deaths than the nuclear bombs dropped on Japan. In passing, he skewers prominent nuclear terrorism and nuclear war alarmists who have been purveying "worst case scenario fantasies." He goes after their insistence that we immediately put their solutions at the top of the national security agenda, and their introduction of extravagant language that has now fed into the political discourse. Mueller calls then-presidential candidate Senator Barack Obama

---

1. See John Mueller, "'At All Costs': The Destructive Consequences of Antiproliferation Policy," in this volume.

on his limitless promise (to an American Israel Public Affairs Committee conference) to do "everything" within his power to stop Iran from getting the bomb, and Senator John McCain matching it by saying it had to be done "at all costs," with neither explaining what "everything" and "at all cost" could lead to. Mueller suggests that one way to reduce incentives for "errant regimes" to take interest in the bomb is to stop threatening them.

In short, there is much to like. But he goes too far. He seems to acknowledge that himself. He writes that no country has found the weapons *particularly* useful. The spread of the weapons is not *necessarily* desirable. Further spread is *unlikely* to accelerate or prove a major danger. The trouble is that for most people, putting nuclear war in the "unlikely" category still leaves a lot to worry about.

But Mueller goes on to dismiss such concerns and conclude that proliferation hardly matters at all, that up to now its effects have been benign, whereas efforts to restrain it do more harm than good. So let us focus mainly on that.

Has the Bomb Made A Significant Impact on the World?

One is almost ashamed to ask the question. Anyone who has lived through the rough parts of the Cold War, or is old enough to remember jumping under his desk during what was then called an atomic drill, has no doubt that it did, in ways both large and small. I will pass over the enormous size and expense of the nuclear weapons enterprise to mention a few items related to life in the United States: The Manhattan Project was, as Annie Jacobsen recently wrote, the mother of all black programs.[2] That precedent plus the Cold War justified the existence of a vast secret national security state, some aspects of which we are just beginning to learn about. That secret world required vetting the "loyalty" of large numbers

---

2. Annie Jacobsen, *Area 51, An Uncensored History of America's Top Secret Military Base* (New York: Little, Brown and Company, 2011).

of people, which implies unprecedented intrusions into their private lives. We have gotten so used to this we think it's normal, but it's a long way from what was considered normal in pre-World War II times. The bomb, plus means for intercontinental delivery in minutes, also changed the U.S. Constitution, shifting the power to initiate war to the president and away from Congress, and therefore away from the democratic process.

We had a lot of close calls during the decades of the Cold War, some of which could conceivably have led to nuclear war. There were quite a number of highly placed U.S. officials who counseled use of the bomb, and in fact were ready to take the president and the country over the cliff to achieve their Cold War aims.[3] Fortunately, reason prevailed. Or the taboo against nuclear use was sufficiently intimidating. Adding to the dangers in the early days of the Cold War, there were no independently controlled locks on the nuclear weapons. Harold Agnew tells of visiting a U.S. air base in Germany and seeing nuclear-armed German planes lined up ready to go. U.S. physical control over the weapons consisted of a single U.S. sentry. The Strategic Air Command (SAC) was very aggressive during this time, flying mock nuclear attacks not only up to the Soviet borders but also inside those borders to get data on Soviet radars. Some U.S. planes were shot down with loss of aircrews. We were very lucky to get through that time unscathed, or perhaps more accurately, un-irradiated.

We know less about how close other countries came to using nuclear weapons, but it appears that at one point in the 1973 Yom Kippur War, Israeli Prime Minister Golda Meir was the only one that stood between Israel's bomb and its use on the battle field.

There were also serious accidents with bombs. Some were inadvertently dropped from planes. The most spectacular incident occurred

---

3. I recall a 1964 briefing by the Director of the Livermore Lab on "civilian" use of the bomb—Project Plowshare. He explained that the real reason for pursuing such projects was to get the US public used to nuclear explosions so that in wartime the president will release their use.

over Goldsboro, N.C. A plane carrying megaton bombs broke up in mid-air, dropping its bombs. They had multiple sequential locks to prevent unintentional or accidental nuclear detonation. The arming sequence on one four-megaton bomb passed through five of its six locks on impact, and the bomb failed to detonate only because the last one held. Had the thermonuclear weapon exploded, a good part of North Carolina would have been flattened, and if the wind had then been blowing north, much of the Eastern coast would have been heavily contaminated with radioactivity. Again, we were very lucky. One should add that all these locks were put on the weapons over the considerable resistance of the Air Force, which worried more about the bombs failing to go off when they were supposed to than having them go off accidentally.

Was the Bomb Useful to Its Owners?

The usefulness of the bomb—or bombs, as others have them, too— is a more complicated question. The first two nuclear bombs ended the war with Japan more quickly than it otherwise would have. The price America paid for this was the eternal onus for being the first to use this new energy source to kill large numbers of people. Without the experience of the Manhattan Project would others have developed the bomb? Once uranium fission was understood in 1939 many scientists around the world understood the possibility of nuclear weapons. The Manhattan Project was, after all, hurried in fear of a German bomb. But probably without the U.S. effort the development elsewhere would have been slower. Recall, however, that most of the World War II effort was in producing the nuclear explosives, highly enriched uranium and plutonium. Commercial nuclear programs now make that easy for possessors of uranium enrichment plants and plutonium separation, or reprocessing, plants.

The bomb didn't do much for the United States in the few years it had a monopoly. And once the Soviets exploded theirs, it was pretty much a standoff. There wasn't much you could do with it, but you didn't want to be without it if Soviet Premier Joseph Stalin had it. In time the weapon took on a life of its own. We built them, and they built them. One thing we know, the bomb was constantly on the mind of leaders.

It was U.S. policy to rely on nuclear weapons to overcome the disparity in manpower if the Soviets attacked Western Europe and thus to deter such an attack. Years after he was Defense Secretary, Robert McNamara told me that despite our declared policy, he would never have authorized use of U.S. nuclear weapons unless the Soviets used them first. (He said he told no one, including National Security Advisor McGeorge Bundy and President John F. Kennedy, because he didn't want to be thought weak, which in itself says quite a lot.) Whether there was actually any deterrence is problematic. If the Soviets weren't going to attack Western Europe anyhow, there was nothing to deter. Still, in this and other situations, the bomb owners saw, and see, it differently than outside observers.

The participants in the Cuban Missile Crisis thought that we came close to nuclear war, and subsequent disclosures about the presence of Soviet battlefield nuclear weapons only underlined that conclusion. The possibilities for disastrous mistakes were considerable, as top officials did not have the degree of control they thought they had. In the 1990s, in an interval between sessions of an international meeting I happened to be standing with two or three others to whom Secretary McNamara was explaining how dangerous the situation was on a particular Saturday. One of those present had been in SAC's Omaha "tank" on that day, and proceeded to tell a stunned McNamara what really went on there on that day. It was the first he'd heard about it.

There is no question that nuclear weapons confer status, both to the countries possessing them, and to the individuals directly involved with them. It's no accident that the five permanent members of the United Nations Security Council are nuclear-armed. Whether the bomb actually does them any good beyond that status at this point is doubtful. But none of them are in any hurry to give it up. Even the Socialists in France and the Laborites in Britain, who when out of power talked of giving up nuclear weapons, quickly changed their mind when they gained power. And bureaucratic prestige is undoubtedly a factor in our still keeping our land-based missiles on alert.

India and Pakistan are if anything increasing their stockpiles. India has plans to outfit submarines with strategic missiles. Israel, too, would presumably insist its nuclear weapons were useful, that is, if they ever admitted they had them. North Korea now brags about its nuclear bombs. And of course the Obama Administration is committing hundreds of billions to upgrade its nuclear weapons complex.[4] So whatever we may think of the nuclear weapons situation, and the seeming uselessness of it all (which could also be said of most military expenditures), the owners are not about to take advice from academic kibitzers.

Have Those Who Have Given Up the Bomb Regretted it?

In support of the unilateral divestment of nuclear weapons, the claim is made that countries that have given up the weapons have not suffered for it and don't regret it. A respectable argument can certainly be made for giving up nuclear weapons.[5] But the expe-

---

4. See William J. Broad and David E. Sanger, "U.S. Ramping Up Major Renewal in Nuclear Arms," *New York Times*, September 21, 2014. There is a delicious irony in this being ordered by a Nobel Peace Prize Laureate.

5. See, especially, Paul Nitze, "A Threat Mostly to Ourselves," *New York Times*, October 28, 1999. Nitze wrote (emphasis added):

> The fact is, I see no compelling reason why we should not *unilaterally* get rid of our nuclear weapons. To maintain them is costly and adds nothing to our security.

> I can think of no circumstances under which it would be wise

rience of countries that have done so is not of much relevance. In reality, only South Africa gave them up, and it only had a few warheads of rudimentary design that weren't of much use in South Africa's military situation, that is, the situation of the former white-only government. The elimination of the weapons took place in unique circumstances—moving from a white to black government—and was a condition for joining the Nuclear Nonproliferation Treaty (NPT) and good standing in the world community. It is doubtful that the other countries sometimes listed in the former nuclear weapon state category—the former Soviet republics on whose territory nuclear weapons remained after the breakup of the Soviet Union—were ever really nuclear states. It's true they relinquished the weapons on their soil, or were bribed to do so, but it does not appear they ever had the ability to use them.

Have Nonproliferation Efforts Caused Great Harm?

The Nonproliferation Efforts Before 1974

Which brings us to the efforts, since the bomb's invention, to keep it within few hands, so-called nonproliferation, and the issue of whether these efforts, especially recent ones, have been on balance harmful. A brief examination of the history of attempts at international nuclear controls shows this is not a sustainable proposition. The fact is, they haven't been potent enough to be harmful. Rather, we have suffered from the lack of adequate international protection against militarizing nuclear energy.

---

for the United States to use nuclear weapons, even in retaliation for their prior use against us. What, for example, would our targets be? It is impossible to conceive of a target that could be hit without large-scale destruction of many innocent people.

I have to say I cannot think of any such circumstances, either.

The starting point in the effort to control what was then called the atom, was the U.S. proposal, based on the 1946 Acheson-Lilienthal Report, for international development of nuclear energy. The central idea was international ownership of what the Report called dangerous nuclear facilities. The Report grasped the essential problem of the dual potential of nuclear energy, but was unfortunately deeply flawed in its specific proposals.[6] In any case, the US proposal had no chance of acceptance by Stalin's Soviet Union, and indeed went nowhere. The United States then did its best to maintain tight security over nuclear technology.

Once the Soviets and the British exploded bombs, we changed course. President Eisenhower launched Atoms for Peace, which amounted to a huge giveaway of nuclear technology to gain political advantage and to create a market for US commercial nuclear reactors and fuel under minimal international controls.[7] In fact, U.S. President Dwight Eisenhower explained that initially no "onerous" controls would be needed because the exported facilities would be too small to worry about. We sponsored the creation of the International Atomic Energy Agency, principally as a distributor of our largesse. The Agency included an inspectorate whose real function was to provide a patina of legitimacy to international nuclear trade, the underlying notion being to avoid any need for our own inspection of customers and any resentment that might provoke. It was not a serious inspection system, rather more a matter of inspectors making friendly visits to their colleagues in the field.

President Kennedy took the spread of nuclear weapons more seriously. Among other things, he pressed Israel to allow inspection of its French-supplied Dimona facility, already suspected of beings a

---

6. For example, it was based on the notion that moderately irradiated plutonium cannot be used for bombs and was thus in the "safe" category, which is false, and in fact was known to be false at the time.

7. The second largest group of participating scientists and engineers (after Britain) came from India.

weapons facility.[8] Kennedy's observation that there could soon be a couple of dozen nuclear states is often described, in view of the present nine, as an example of undue alarm.[9] It was not a prediction; it was a warning, which led to a number of steps that slowed the spread of the bomb, starting with the 1968 Nuclear Nonproliferation Treaty.

The draft treaty started out as an effort by states without nuclear weapons to protect themselves by mutually agreeing not to obtain them. In the lengthy negotiations, however, other features got added that changed its character, most particularly a promise, summed up in the oft-quoted phrase "inalienable right," to access nuclear technology on a non-discriminatory basis, so long as they were subject to International Atomic Energy Agency (IAEA) inspections. As the treaty was then interpreted, this included uranium enrichment and separation of plutonium, the technologies that offer access to nuclear explosives. The treaty barred countries beyond the original five weapons states from getting bombs, but had no explicit limits on how close such a country could come to a bomb without violating the treaty.

U.S. President Richard Nixon, while cool to the treaty that had been signed by his predecessor, U.S. President Lyndon Johnson, nevertheless sent it the Senate for ratification after deciding that it did not in any way reduce his freedom of action with respect to U.S. nuclear weapons. Most notably, that included sharing them

---

8. Under Atoms for Peace the United States had donated a small research reactor to Israel and signed a peaceful uses agreement. The US-supplied facility proved a useful vehicle for educating Israel's nuclear weapons scientists.

9. "There are indications because of new inventions, that 10, 15, or 20 nations will have a nuclear capacity, including Red China, by the end of the Presidential office in 1964. This is extremely serious. . . I think the fate not only of our own civilization, but I think the fate of world and the future of the human race, is involved in preventing a nuclear war." "The Third Kennedy-Nixon Presidential Debate," Debate Transcript, *Commission on Presidential Debates*, October 13, 1960, available from *www.debates.org/index.php?page=october-13-1960-debate-transcript.*

with the North Atlantic Treaty Organization. He gave instructions to his administration's officials that they were not to press countries to sign, especially West Germany. The country did sign, as did Japan, and ultimately nearly all countries—but that was later.

The first test of U.S. application of the treaty came in 1969, immediately after ratification. The United States had been aware that Israel had been conducting a secret nuclear weapons program since the 1950s. It already had built some nuclear weapons, although the United States wasn't sure about this. The U.S. State and Defense departments wanted to withhold the advanced F-4 aircraft Israel wanted in return for restrictions on Israel's manufacture of nuclear weapons, a position that carried over from the Johnson administration.[10] U.S. National Security Advisor Henry Kissinger was still hoping to get Israel's signature on the NPT. (His cynical—but not entirely wrong—observation was that this would be worthwhile, even though even though he expected Israel to maintain a clandestine weapons program, because it would be a smaller one than otherwise.) The State Department offered to come up with a favorable legal opinion on treaty compliance if Israel would stay "a screwdriver turn away." But when it came to President Nixon's September 1969 meeting with Israel's prime minister, Golda Meir, none of this mattered. He let it all go. What he mainly cared about was that Israel support him in the Cold War, and especially in Vietnam. Since it served neither party's interests to publicize them, Israeli nuclear weapons became a non-subject in the U.S. Government, and the NPT was relegated to its place off to the side.

It's worth remembering that during those years, nonproliferation was regarded in the foreign policy and defense establishments as a kind of side show handled by intellectual officials who were not considered weighty enough or tough enough to perform in the main ring—the Cold War. (To jump ahead, it was only after the demise

---

10. Just before he left office, President Johnson had overridden the departments to permit the F-4 sale. But in allowing it the Defense Department wrote in conditions that in effect left the final decision to the Nixon administration.

of the Soviet Union that the U.S. Defense Department, desperately searching for budget justifications, acquired more respect for non-proliferation, or rather counter-proliferation, which is its more expensive cousin.)

The Nonproliferation Efforts Post-1974

There was considerable consternation after the 1974 Indian bomb test, which turned out to be a pivotal event in U.S. nonproliferation policy.[11] It became evident to all that a country with access to reprocessing, and thus plutonium, could easily produce nuclear bombs. Once a country had ready access to nuclear explosives—highly enriched uranium and plutonium—IAEA inspections (optimistically labeled "safeguards") could no longer be relied upon to provide warning of a shift to weapons. To prevent easy access to nuclear weapons there needed to be restrictions on the technologies that produced these explosives—enrichment and reprocessing. At the initiative of the United States, the main nuclear technology exporters formed the Nuclear Suppliers Group (NSG) in 1975 to put some brakes on such exports.

At first the arrangement functioned sub rosa because on the face of it, it is at odds with the extravagant interpretation of the "inalienable right" language in the NPT, and the United States and other exporters shied away from taking on the argument. In fact, the opposite is true. Only with some technology controls could the IAEA inspections provide the "safeguards" protection that the treaty requires.

In this post-Indian bomb phase the United States succeeded in preventing several reprocessing exports from Europe to Asian countries. In 1976 U.S. President Gerald Ford announced that the Unit-

---

11. The immediate Nixon administration reaction was rather different. In a cable from the Middle East, Secretary of State Kissinger warned his surprised staff against any strong reaction. He was apparently in the process of putting together a nuclear deal of his own that he did not want upset.

ed States would abide by the same nonproliferation restrictions that it asked others to abide by. It would not plan on use of plutonium fuel and would not conduct civilian reprocessing. The nuclear energy community saw this, and still professes to see this, as a limitation on the application of nuclear power. In reality, reprocessing to produce plutonium fuel for current nuclear power plants is grossly uneconomic. So, while avoiding wasteful expenditure was not the prime intention, the restriction on reprocessing saved the United States and other countries a great deal of money. To jump ahead, the same is true of restrictions on enrichment—these have hurt the vanity of some countries, but not their pocketbooks, or their carbon dioxide emissions. There were never any bars to any NPT member country importing nuclear power reactors. Quite to the contrary, the suppliers beat the drums for reactor sales. What held back nuclear power, and still holds it back, was the inability of the industry to turn out an economic product that met safety requirements. The proposition that international nonproliferation policies hobbled the development of nuclear power is therefore entirely untenable.

India's 1974 bomb had other delayed consequences. It became widely known that India produced the plutonium for its bomb in facilities that, although not internationally inspected, were covered by peaceful uses pledges to Canada and the United States. India tried to explain this away by saying its bomb was peaceful.[12] It was too much for Congress to swallow. It became an important impetus for passage of the 1978 Nuclear Non-Proliferation Act, which imposed nonproliferation conditions for nuclear exports, among them that the importer accept IAEA inspections on all its nuclear facili-

---

12. This was a flagrant disregard by India of the obvious meaning of the peaceful uses pledges. But it is also true that the U.S. Atomic Energy Commission had provided some footing for this argument by supporting Project Plowshare to develop "peaceful nuclear explosions," mainly as a way of putting a friendly face on the AEC's nuclear weapons activities. The project was initiated in 1961 not terminated until 1977. The international publicity in favor of PNEs led to the inclusion of an article in the NPT covering the provision of such services internationally. It has become a dead letter, but caused considerable damage to nonproliferation along the way.

ties.

Has Nonproliferation Caused Loss of Life?

John Mueller makes the claim that nonproliferation policy caused
more deaths than the Hiroshima and Nagasaki explosions, by
which he is referring to the 2003 U.S. invasion of Iraq. He is right
about the effect of the 2003 invasion, but it would be a considerable stretch to count the invasion in the nonproliferation column. In
an oft-cited 2003 Vanity Fair interview with U.S. Deputy Defense
Secretary Paul Wolfowitz, he cites eliminating "weapons of mass
destruction," not as the real reason for the U.S. invasion, but as
the politically convenient reason.[13] It was, as we have learned, an
outright lie that the Bush administration had significant evidence
pointing to Iraqi nuclear weapons.[14] In any case, the invasion was
named Operation IRAQI FREEDOM, which points in a different
direction, one relating to control of the Middle East.

A related question is whether nonproliferation-inspired Iraqi sanctions in the decade preceding the 2003 invasion resulted in the
deaths of large numbers of Iraqis, especially children. That there
were many deaths as a consequence does not seem to be at issue,
although there is not agreement on the numbers. In a famous 1996
CBS interview, Lesley Stahl asked U.S. Secretary of State Madeleine Albright about the effect of U.S. sanctions against Iraq: "We

---

13. U.S. Deputy Secretary of Defense Paul Wolfowitz, Interview with Sam Tannenhaus, *Vanity Fair*, May 9, 2003, transcript available from *www.defense.gov/
transcripts/transcript.aspx?transcriptid=2594.*

14. A few days after the start of the March 2003 invasion, I found myself at
a security conference seated next to the visibly nervous director of the CIA's
Weapons Intelligence, Nonproliferation, and Arms Control Center. He said if
the invading force does not find any evidence of nuclear, biological, or chemical weapons he is going to lose his job. But, he said hopefully, he was sure they
will find something in a desk drawer in Baghdad. It does not seem we had much
evidence going in, or that this could have been the real reason for doing so. The
man left his job soon after.

have heard that a half million children have died. I mean, that's more children than died in Hiroshima. And, you know, is the price worth it?" Madeleine Albright's chilling reply was: "I think this is a very hard choice, but the price—we think the price is worth it."[15] Again, there's no denying the consequences. The question is whether they had much to do with nonproliferation, or were simply part of an effort to hem in Iraqi President Saddam Hussein.

Mueller raises the same point with respect to sanctions against North Korea. Here, if anything, the reasons for sanctions are even more complex than in the case of Iraq, as is the relationship of the sanctions to the misery of the non-privileged population.[16] It should be remembered that the initial reaction of the Clinton administration to North Korea's refusal in 1992 of key IAEA inspections (and therefore of the NPT) was to make the country an extraordinarily generous offer, which after the conclusion of negotiations in 1994 was known as the Agreed Framework. The North Koreans agreed to shut down their small plutonium production reactor and stop building two larger but still relatively small reactors; the United States agreed to shield them from their NPT violation by getting the IAEA to agree to postpone the disputed inspections. In the meantime North Korea would receive (from South Korea and Japan) two large light water reactors worth about $5 billion. In addition the North received a large supply of oil. The deal did not make sense, and fell apart when it became obvious that North Korea was not keeping to its terms.[17] But the point for our purposes here is that

15. U.S. Secretary of State Madeleine Albright, Interview with Lesley Stahl, *60 Minutes*, originally aired May 12, 1996. Albright later said what she said was stupid, which of course it was, as it played badly.

16. In a strange twist, when the Clinton administration hoped to make headway with North Korea, the ever-enthusiastic Secretary Albright showed up in Pyongyang at an October 22, 2000 celebration for Kim Jong-il, and put on an embarrassingly gushing performance. See Jane Perlez, "Albright Greeted with a Fanfare by North Korea," *New York Times*, October 24, 2000.

17. Aside from the questionable aspect of rewarding flagrant violation of the NPT, in effect submitting to blackmail, the arrangement made no sense from a

U.S. nonproliferation policy in this instance could not have been more generous.

What Does Current U.S. Nonproliferation Policy Really Amount to?

U.S. nonproliferation policy is far from the strict system (let alone overly strict system) that it is made out to be by the nuclear community in its frequent complaints. There are two aspects to it: The first is the broad effort conducted mainly at mid-levels in the State Department, working through the IAEA and other agencies, and ostensibly based on the NPT; the second, in many ways the more important, is conducted from the top and deals with Iran, and to a limited extent with North Korea.[18]

The broad international effort deliberately takes an incremental and non-confrontational approach to the problem—working to get others to agree to voluntary improvements in the application of IAEA safeguards, for example, or details of export procedures. The officials involved are the ones who go to the IAEA's conferences and meet with corresponding representatives from other supplier states. In practice, their activities amount to nibbling at the issues, and even then subject to the condition that they not disturb the promotion of nuclear power, and especially the possibility of U.S. sales of nuclear power plants.

In this, the Obama administration has outpaced the footsteps of its predecessors. But it is not widely known that this administration

---

technical point of view: The reactors were much too large for the North Korean grid, which could not sustain the power loss from disconnecting one of the large reactors. And the grid was too small to protect the reactors from a safety point of view. Ironically, the plutonium production capacity of the two proposed reactors was larger than that of all the reactors that the North Koreans were supposed to shut down.

18. Doing essentially nothing about North Korea has now been dressed up in State Department language as "strategic patience."

has created a "Team USA," composed of officials from Departments of State, Energy, and Commerce, to promote nuclear power abroad. And there is a designated official on the National Security Council staff to shepherd the effort. It's no wonder that when Congress takes up the nuclear export agreements with potential customers, the State Department invariably testifies in favor of laxer conditions.[19]

To maintain friendly, and especially non-confrontational relations with potential customers, the State Department has gone along with a watering down of the NPT's objectives by describing the treaty as resting on three pillars, only one of which is nonproliferation. The others are nuclear disarmament and, most importantly, development of nuclear energy. And it is said that progress on any of the three depends on progress of the other two. In practical terms it means that the offices charged with trying to rein in proliferation are therefore committed to supporting the expanded worldwide use of nuclear energy, and doing so when we admittedly still don't have a satisfactory way of ensuring that it will not be put to military use.

The diplomats busy themselves with inoffensive solutions, however impractical, the best example being fuel banks, which have become a standard "solution" to the problems posed by national enrichment facilities. It's unlikely that top-level people understand that that a fuel bank makes no economic or engineering sense at all, but it sounds good, and so has become entrenched in nuclear

---

19. The mother of all lax agreements is the one negotiated with India and finalized in 2008. India opposed the NPT from the beginning. It refused comprehensive IAEA inspection of its nuclear facilities and so was barred, by Nuclear Supplier Group guidelines, from receiving nuclear exports. This is the group whose formation we initiated after the 1974 Indian bomb. In the hope of gaining a large amount of nuclear business, the Bush administration waived the export restrictions of thee 1978 NNPA that were put in place in response to the 1974 Indian bomb and pressured the NSG to waive its guidelines. The Bush administration thereby punched a hole in the NPT. As of July 2014, there has yet to be any nuclear business for the United States. The Obama administration later supported fully this policy toward India's nuclear activities.

proliferation boilerplate.[20]

Another way in which nonproliferation has been soft-pedaled is by current shift in emphasis to combating nuclear terrorism by non-state actors as opposed to nuclear weapons development by established states. The diplomatic aspects of combatting terrorism are relatively easy—everyone is against it so one can organize security summits in total agreement.[21] That agreement would be more difficult to obtain if we were talking about the necessary restrictions on the use of nuclear energy to keep it from spilling over into military applications.

The dilution of the effort to stop proliferation of nuclear weapons is further effected by the now-standard inclusion of it in the broader category of proliferation of weapons of mass destruction, which include biological and chemical weapons.[22] Neither of the latter two is remotely as significant as nuclear weapons, but including them blurs the focus on nuclear weapons.

The second aspect of U.S. nonproliferation policy, the one that the president and top officials do take seriously, has to do with mainly constraining Iran's potential nuclear weapons capabilities. The enmity between the United States and Iran goes back to the 1979

20. See, for example, an op-ed by Nuclear Threat Initiative co-chairman, and former senator, Sam Nunn, "Open a Nuclear Fuel Bank," *New York Times*, July 11, 2014. There is a competitive market in fuel. The best guarantee of a fuel supply is a commercial contract. It's easy to create one's own stockpile of enriched. A bank for manufactured fuel is impractical because there are many types of fuel assemblies, with different levels of enrichment, and it would be effectively impossible to stock them all.

21. The purveyors of nuclear terrorism threats have managed to spook top leaders by greatly exaggerating the possibilities. Accounts tell of this fear greatly affecting President Bush after he went through a nuclear bomb scare involving New York and Washington, and President Obama seems equally seized with the issue.

22. To take things to an absurd degree, the legal definition of a weapon of mass destruction (18 U.S. Code § 921 – Definitions) includes explosive charges as small as one-quarter ounce [sic].

Islamic Revolution and the deposing of the Shah.[23] Iran's nuclear program, and an interest in nuclear weapons, also goes back to the time of the Shah. The current U.S. concern about Iran's nuclear capabilities has several elements. There is the obvious worry about Iran's intentions in developing uranium enrichment technology that could give it ready access to large quantities of highly enriched uranium, should it decide to develop nuclear weapons. But other countries have comparable capabilities without drawing the same level of concern. It is difficult to justify—under the NPT, as it has been interpreted for decades—a separate standard for Iran than that applied to other NPT members. The concern over Iran's nuclear capabilities is inextricably tied to fear of the political shadow such capabilities, even if not militarized, may cast over the Middle East and the influence Iran may derive from it.

A clearer way to view what is going on in the negotiations over Iran's nuclear program is to see it as a struggle by the United States and Israel to maintain Israel's nuclear weapons monopoly in the Middle East. If anything sums up the major themes of U.S. non-proliferation policy, it would be protecting against the possibility of nuclear terrorism and protecting Israel's nuclear weapons. The United States has gone so far as to cooperate with Israel in physically sabotaging Iran's uranium enrichment activities.[24] Which is more than a little odd, as it puts the United States in cooperation with a country that resists the NPT norm to enforce NPT discipline on an NPT member suspected of harboring intentions at odds with its treaty obligations.

We never went this far before, but there is a long history to U.S. protection for Israel's putatively secret nuclear weapons, a policy supported even by U.S. politicians who otherwise take a strong

---

23. Many of Iran's nuclear scientists and engineers under the Shah, some of whom are still working in Iran, were trained at MIT under a special program specifically for Iran.

24. Israel went beyond that to assassinate Iranian scientists, without any admonition from the United States.

stand on nonproliferation.[25] The U.S. president still feigns igno-
rance about Israel's nuclear weapons, and the subject is off-limits
even within the government, as it has been since the Nixon administration. It isn't off-limits in the rest of the world and we pay
heavily in terms of international credibility when it comes to nonproliferation. In 2010 the NPT Review Conference unanimously
approved final statement called for a conference on weapons of
mass destruction in the Middle East, to take place in 2012. Immediately after the vote, to which the U.S. representative agreed,
President Obama trashed the notion of such a conference. It has
still not taken place. No one is fooled.

Where Does This Leave Us?

Faced with a history of ineffective and hypocritical nonproliferation policy, should we just let it all go? It turns out there are things
worse than fecklessness and hypocrisy.[26]

---

25. U.S. President Jimmy Carter's White House was famous for its emphasis on
nonproliferation, but hid the fact of Israel's 1979 nuclear test in seas south of Africa, carried out in violation of the Limited Test Ban, to which Israel was a party.
During the previous administration I recall a 1976 dinner honoring Fred Iklé,
then head of the Arms Control and Disarmament Agency. Senator Stuart Symington, the sponsor of the 1976 Symington Amendment (that banned U.S. aid
to countries that deal in nuclear enrichment technology without complying with
IAEA inspections) spoke about the importance of nonproliferation and praised
Iklé for his commitment to it. When he sat down I asked the senator what he
thought about nuclear weapons in Israel. He immediately replied, "They have to
have them, I've been telling Moshe Dayan that for years."

26. In an accompanying article in this volume, "Getting Past Nonproliferation,"
Harvey Sopolsky takes a different tack. Whereas Mueller decries US nonproliferation policy because he thinks nuclear weapons don't matter, Sopolsky opposes
it because he thinks nuclear weapons do matter. He sees nonproliferation as of a
piece with "extended deterrence"—U.S. nuclear guarantees to our allies—which
he doesn't like at all. Better, he says, to let them get their own nuclear weapons.
But what if this abandonment of nonproliferation leads to nuclear weapons in
the hands not only of friends but also of enemies and non-state actors, including those in the Middle East? Sopolsky's less-than-convincing answer is that

The original, perhaps simplistic, logic behind nonproliferation was that as the number of nuclear weapons states increases, the number of strategic relationships among them increases much faster, and it will become extremely difficult to keep the weapons from being used. Henry Kissinger recently reiterated his belief in the validity of this view:

> If one imagines a world of tens of nations with nuclear weapons and major powers trying to balance their own deterrent equations, plus the deterrent equations of the subsystems, deterrence calculation would become impossibly complicated. To assume that, in such a world, nuclear catastrophe could be avoided would be unrealistic.[27]

It would be nice to think that this paints an overly pessimistic picture, and that faced with the potentially awful consequences of the spread of nuclear weapons, and remembering the awfulness of the large wars fought in the last century, people and leaders would keep far away from any possibility of nuclear war. But that view conflicts with history. The horrors of World War I did not prevent World War II twenty years later. The lessons of Vietnam did not prevent our repeating the experience in Iraq and Afghanistan. Wars and aggression are intertwined with domestic politics, and politicians, no matter how bright, have little time or inclination to understand the

---

"deterrence and forensics work." In other words, enemy states will fear to attack the United States. And if they contemplate the risky course of handing bombs to non-state groups who would use them against the United States, they would again be deterred from doing so because "the links are sure to be revealed." In a way Sopolsky is saying if we just abandon nonproliferation, in fact, if we encourage the opposite, we won't have to worry about nuclear weapons in the rest of the world. Let us just say it is a provocative argument.

27. Henry Kissinger, foreword in Graham Allison, et al. "Nuclear Proliferation: Risk and Responsibility," Triangle Paper 60, (Washington, DC: Trilateral Commission, 2006), v.

issues.[28] That is even truer when there is a technical component, or when the consequences are likely to be delayed, a state of affairs that is ever present when dealing with nuclear issues. It's well to recall that President Eisenhower's Atoms for Peace program of the 1950s set much of the configuration of present-day nuclear programs around the world. Soon after he announced it Soviet Foreign Minister Molotov asked U.S. Secretary of State John Foster Dulles why the United States wanted to spread nuclear weapons capabilities through the program. Dulles had no idea what Molotov was talking about and when he returned to Washington asked his assistant Gerard Smith to confirm that Molotov was talking nonsense. Smith had to explain to the astonished Dulles that Molotov had a point. We should not assume that today's top-level politicians around the world are brighter or wiser than their predecessors. And in crises all bets are off.

Insofar as nuclear energy programs are concerned, the only thing that makes sense from a security point of view is to seek a healthy margin between nuclear energy activities and any possible military applications, and to maintain as best we can the taboo on nuclear weapon use. As tattered as it is, the NPT is all that we have as a rallying banner. In the end this will work only if we all agree on common standards. Holding back the spread of the bomb—and, in fact, rolling back the bomb—remain important objectives.

---

28. In a talk at the RAND Corporation in Santa Monica before Secretary Kissinger assumed his role in the Nixon administration he said, "Never underestimate the superficiality of important people."

CHAPTER 5

The Next Nuclear War

Matthew Kroenig and Rebecca Davis Gibbons[1]

Since the United States dropped atomic bombs on Japan at the close of World War II, world leaders have had the wisdom to avoid another nuclear war. Humanity witnessed the terrifyingly destructive power of nuclear weapons at Hiroshima and Nagasaki and vowed never to repeat the mistake. The Cold War superpowers set up effective international systems to control the spread of nuclear technology and prevent the proliferation of nuclear weapons to additional countries. While there are a handful of states that possess nuclear weapons today, none of them are run by leaders so irrational or suicidal as to intentionally launch a nuclear attack. Moreover, these countries have put in place prudent policies and technologies to prevent an accidental or unauthorized nuclear launch. The upshot of these developments is that nuclear weapons have not been used in seventy years and we have little reason to fear that they will ever be used again.

This line of thinking is certainly comforting, but is it correct? The fact is that nuclear weapons and international conflict continue to exist. The number of nuclear-armed states has slowly grown over time and, outside of the United States and Europe, the nuclear powers are increasing the size and sophistication of their nuclear

1. Matthew Kroenig is an Associate Professor in the Department of Government and School of Foreign Service and a Senior Fellow at the Brent Scowcroft Center on International Security. Rebecca Davis Gibbons is a Visiting Assistant Professor in the Department of Government at Bowdoin College.

arsenals, as well as their reliance on nuclear weapons in military doctrine and strategy. Indeed, recent years have seen an increase in overt nuclear threats by some leaders. Political tensions remain among nuclear powers and in many regions of the world these conflicts are becoming more intense. In addition, poorly safeguarded nuclear material around the globe could find its way to extremist organizations that could use nuclear weapons as an instrument of terror. While the risk of nuclear war on any given day is low, *it is not zero*. And this risk must be multiplied across many nuclear-armed actors and international conflicts for years to come. In sum, there is a frighteningly real risk that humanity has not witnessed its last nuclear war.

This article will examine the prospects for the next nuclear war. It will begin by defining our key concept: nuclear use. Next, it will review the first and only instance of nuclear use, the dropping of atomic bombs on Hiroshima and Nagasaki in World War II, to assess whether the pathway to the first and only existing case of nuclear use might be repeated. It then articulates the theoretical processes that could give rise to nuclear war as identified in the international relations and nuclear deterrence literatures. Next, in order to identify the flashpoints that could result in the next nuclear exchange, it examines the most salient geopolitical rivalries between nuclear-armed actors in the world today. Finally, it offers concluding remarks regarding the steps world leaders can take to prevent future nuclear wars.

Defining Nuclear Use

We begin by defining a key term: nuclear use. We define nuclear use as the detonation of a nuclear weapon against an enemy target. Some U.S. Department of Defense officials declare that "Nuclear weapons are used every day," to emphasize that nuclear weapons play an important and enduring role in maintaining strategic deterrence and keeping the peace.[2] Similarly, scholars have explored the deterrent, coercive, and symbolic effects of nuclear weapons.[3] We do not mean nuclear use in this sense. We also exclude from our definition nuclear tests or nuclear demonstration shots that could be used for political effect, but that do not result in death or destruction. Rather, for the purposes of this chapter, nuclear use is defined as a nuclear attack resulting in physical damage of enemy targets.

Nuclear Use in World War II

When considering the next use of nuclear weapons, the most logical place to begin is the last and only instance of nuclear use, the U.S. atomic bombing of Japan at the end of World War II. Understanding U.S. President Harry Truman's decision to employ nuclear weapons in warfare may shed some light on why leaders might consider nuclear use in the future.

On August 6, 1945, the United States dropped an atomic bomb on Hiroshima and, three days later, on August 9, a second weapon was used against Nagasaki. Almost seventy years after the event, his-

---

2. For example, former U.S. Defense Secretary James Schlesinger makes this point in Melanie Kirkpatrick's article, "Why We Don't Want a Nuclear-Free World," *Wall Street Journal*, July 13, 2009, available from *www.wsj.com/articles/SB124726489588925407*.

3. See, for example, Matthew Kroenig, "Nuclear Superiority and the Balance of Resolve: Explaining Nuclear Crisis Outcomes," *International Organization* 67, No. 1 (January 2013): 141-171; Glenn Snyder and Paul Diesing, *Conflict Among Nations: Bargaining, Decision-Making, and System Structure in International Crises* (Princeton, NJ: Princeton University Press, 1977); Richard Betts, *Nuclear Blackmail and Nuclear Coercion* (Washington, DC: Brookings Institution Press, 1987); Marc Trachtenberg, *History and Strategy* (Princeton, NJ: Princeton University Press, 1991); Kyle Beardsley and Victor Asal, "Winning with the Bomb," *The Journal of Conflict Resolution* 53, No. 2 (April 2009): 278-301; Carol Atkinson, "Using nuclear weapons," *Review of International Studies* 36 (2010): 839–851; and R. Davis Gibbons, "Signals Intelligence? The Effectiveness of Nuclear and Non-Nuclear Signals in a Crisis" (Washington, DC: Center for Strategic and International Studies, 2012).

torians continue to debate the motivations behind Truman's deci-sion.[4] According to the traditional account, the United States used nuclear weapons to quickly conclude the war in the Pacific and save the lives of many American GIs (and Japanese soldiers and civilians) that would have been lost if Washington had pursued the alternative route of a ground invasion of the Japanese islands. Ac-cording to a more recent revisionist view, the nuclear weapons were not in fact necessary to force a Japanese surrender because Tokyo was nearly ready to capitulate and the Soviet Union's impending entrance into the Pacific War would have been more than enough to force Japan to concede defeat.[5] Rather, according to this perspec-tive, Truman's use of nuclear weapons was aimed not at Tokyo, but at Moscow. By using nuclear weapons, Truman was able to end the war quickly enough to prevent Soviet forces from occupying large portions of East Asia and to demonstrate America's awesome new military capability to its future Cold War rival.

Our purpose here is not to adjudicate between these interpretations, nor to improve upon the existing debate, but rather to ask what this historical event might tell us about future nuclear use. If Truman were motivated to quickly end a costly conventional war as the traditional account would have us believe, then there is reason to suspect that such processes could re-occur. Desperate times call for desperate measures and it is conceivable that a nuclear-armed state could be tempted to use nuclear weapons in a future attempt to staunch the bloodletting from a drawn-out conventional conflict. Indeed, as we will see below, some states in the world today active-ly plan to use nuclear weapons early in warfare as a way to offset the conventional superiority of potential adversaries.

---

4. For a summary of the differing narratives surrounding this decision, see Bar-ton J. Bernstein, "Truman and the A-Bomb: Targeting Noncombatants, Using the Bomb, and His Defending the 'Decision," *The Journal of Military History* 62, No. 3 (July 1998): 547-570.

5. Gar Alperovitz, *Atomic Diplomacy: Hiroshima and Potsdam* (New York: Si-mon and Schuster, 1965) is one of the most well-known books to make this controversial claim.

It is also possible that states might use nuclear weapons in the future in order to demonstrate their capabilities to potential adversaries. If Hiroshima and Nagasaki were primarily about revealing a revolutionary new military capability, then this case is less instructive as no adversary is likely to need that message again. After all, Hiroshima and Nagasaki and the hundreds of nuclear tests that followed provided sufficient proof of concept. In this way the first nuclear use may have been idiosyncratic because it was the first.

If, however, Hiroshima and Nagasaki can be interpreted as a warning shot to a potential future enemy about possessing both the ability and the will to go nuclear, then it may be more relevant. It is possible that future decisions to use nuclear weapons could include a consideration of secondary and tertiary effects, such as demonstrating resolve to other states or deterring or otherwise precluding other parties from intervening in an ongoing conflict.

One must be cautious, however, about extrapolating from a single data point and this single episode, no matter how important, cannot be the only input into our study on the future of nuclear use. To broaden our perspective, therefore, we next turn to theory.

Theories of Nuclear Use

International relations scholars and nuclear deterrence theorists have identified several possible processes by which nuclear war could occur. The most prominent of these scenarios are reviewed here, including: irrational nuclear use, accidental nuclear use, inadvertent nuclear use, catalytic nuclear war, nuclear use against non-nuclear opponents, splendid first strike, use 'em or lose 'em, brinkmanship, and limited nuclear use.

Irrational Nuclear Use

The first potential cause of nuclear use is irrationality. In practice, irrational nuclear use means a leader using nuclear weapons in pursuit of goals that are so vastly different from our own as to be utterly unrecognizable. Political scientists tend to assume that states are unified rational actors that value their continued existence above all else, but this is a simplifying assumption, not a description of the world in which we actually live.[6] Historically, there have been rare leaders who have been willing to destroy their own states in the pursuit of broader ideological goals, including Adolf Hitler in World War II.[7] One could similarly imagine a leader of a nuclear-armed state on the losing end of a major war, deciding that he has nothing left to lose and voluntarily choosing to unleash the destructive force of nuclear weapons. For example, if the North Korean regime were to collapse, might North Korean supreme leader Kim Jung-Un decide to use nuclear weapons, figuring that if he is going down he might as well take everyone else with him?

Alternatively, it is at least conceivable that somewhere someday a leader could ascend to power with religious, nationalist, racist, or some other extremist worldview that causes him to value nuclear destruction over self-preservation. Iran's clerical establishment, for example, contains a minority of individuals who genuinely appear to hold millenarian religious beliefs.[8] If Iran acquires nuclear weapons and one of these leaders comes to have his finger on the nuclear trigger, it is at least imaginable that he might try to launch an unprovoked nuclear attack in an attempt to bring about an apocalypse. Granted, this type of nuclear use may be the most

---

6. Kenneth N. Waltz, "Reflections on Theory of International Politics: a response to my critics," in *Neorealism and its Critics*, Robert O. Keohane, ed. (New York: Columbia University Press, 1986), 330–331.

7. David F. Lindenfeld, "The Prevalence of Irrational Thinking in the Third Reich: Notes toward the Reconstruction of Modern Value Rationality," *Central European History* 30, No. 3 (1997): 365-385.

8. See for example Jeffrey Herf's "Taking Iran's Anti-Semitism Seriously," *The National Interest*, June 2, 2014 or Mehdi Khalaji's "Apocalyptic Politics: On the Rationality of Iranian Policy," *Policy Focus,* 79 (Washington, DC: The Washington Institute, January 2008).

farfetched of those discussed in this chapter, but many international events, including the terrorist attacks of 9/11 and the recent global financial crisis, were virtually unimaginable until they happened.

Accidental Nuclear Use

A second type of potential nuclear use can be characterized as accidental or unintentional. In 1982 the U.S. Department of Defense (DoD) catalogued all previously known nuclear accidents from 1950 to the 1980s.[9] The list included the 1982 Titan II crisis in which a dropped wrench socket in a nuclear missile silo nearly caused a nuclear explosion, and a number of cases in which aircraft carrying nuclear weapons crashed or dropped nuclear weapons into the ocean but that fortunately failed to detonate.[10]

Scott Sagan, in his book, *The Limits of Safety*, catalogs a number of near nuclear accidents during the Cold War period, including a 1966 midair collision between a B-52 bomber and a KC-135 tanker that led to the release of four hydrogen bombs near Palomares, Spain.[11] In 1968, a B-52 bomber on airborne alert caught fire over Greenland near a U.S. early warning site, causing four one-megaton thermonuclear bombs to hurtle toward the ground.[12] The current era is not immune from nuclear accidents, including the 2007 incident in which nuclear weapons were accidentally and unknowingly transported from Minot Air Force Base in North Dakota to

---

9. Department of Defense, "Narrative Summaries of Accidents Involving U.S. Nuclear Weapons, 1950-1980," April 1981, available from *nsarchive.files.wordpress.com/2010/04/635.pdf*.

10. Eric Schlosser, *Command and Control: Nuclear Weapons, the Damascus Accident, and the Illusion of Safety* (New York: The Penguin Press, 2013).

11. Scott Sagan, *The Limits of Safety, Princeton* (NJ: Princeton University Press, 1993), 178.

12. Ibid.

Barksdale Air Force Base in Louisiana.[13] Other nuclear weapons
states have also had their share of incidents[14] and newer nuclear
weapons states may be even more prone to accidents, especially as
they strive to develop stable command and control structures.[15] In
none of these cases did the nuclear warhead detonate, but we might
not be so lucky next time.

Inadvertent Nuclear Use

An inadvertent nuclear use would occur if a nuclear-capable state
decides to launch a nuclear war under the incorrect belief that it
is already under nuclear attack.[16] Perhaps the most sophisticated
theoretical discussion of inadvertent war is provided by Thomas
Schelling in his discussion of "reciprocal fear of surprise attack."[17]
Schelling argues that when two nuclear adversaries face each other
in crisis, each side may rightly worry that the other side is considering nuclear attack. If there is an advantage to striking first, then, in
these difficult circumstances under intense time pressures, a cycle
of fear could lead to nuclear war. As Schelling writes, "Fear that
the other may be about to strike in the mistaken belief that we are
about to strike gives us a motive for striking, and so justifies the

13. "Flight of Nuclear Warheads Over U.S. Is Under Inquiry," *New York Times*,
September 6, 2007.

14. On British nuclear weapons accidents, see Eric Schlosser, "Nuclear weapons: an accident waiting to happen," *Guardian* (Manchester), September 13,
2013.

15. Peter D. Feaver, "Command and Control in Emerging Nuclear Nations,"
International Security 17, No. 3 (Winter 1992-93): 160-187.

16. In his book, *The Logic of Accidental Nuclear War* (Washington, DC: Brookings Institution Press, 1993), Bruce G. Blair discusses a number of ways in
which accidental nuclear war could be launched in the post-Cold War era due to
risks in the U.S. and Russian command and control systems.

17. Thomas Schelling, *The Strategy of Conflict* (Cambridge, MA: Harvard University Press, 1960), 207.

other's motive."[18]

In *The Limits of Safety*, Sagan provides several examples of near-inadvertent nuclear war during the Cuban Missile Crisis. In one episode, an intruder—later identified as a bear—led to the sounding of a "sabotage alarm," which set off similar alarms at all the bases in the area. At one base, an incorrectly wired alarm sent pilots of nuclear-armed fighter aircraft to prepare for takeoff before a car raced down the runway to stop them.[19] Also during the crisis, Vandenberg Air Force Base conducted a regularly scheduled ballistic missile test that the Soviet Union might have reasonably misread as a nuclear missile launch.[20] Finally, at the end of the crisis, Moorestown, New Jersey radar operators alerted NORAD that an incoming missile attack was underway when a training tape simulating an attack was mistakenly run in their system.[21]

Inadvertent nuclear war nearly occurred again in the 1983 ABLE ARCHER incident, in which a very realistic North Atlantic Treaty Organization (NATO) military exercise during a period of tension led the Soviets to worry the training operation was a cover for war preparations. The Soviets put their own nuclear forces on alert in response.[22] A similar scare occurred in in the post-Cold War era in January 1995 when a U.S.-Norwegian weather balloon was launched from Norway to study the Aurora Borealis. A Russian early warning radar detected this object, leading Russian President Boris Yeltsin to activate his "nuclear keys" for the first time. Eventually radars detected that the balloon was going out to sea

---

18. Ibid., 207.

19. Sagan, *The Limits of Safety*, 98-100.

20. Ibid., 78-80.

21. Ibid., 130-131.

22. For declassified documents on the ABLE ARCHER Exercise, see National Security Archive "The Able Archer 83 Sourcebook," November 7, 2013, available from *www2.gwu.edu/~nsarchiv/nukevault/ablearcher/*.

and Russian forces stood down.[23] Given the frequency with which countries have feared themselves to be under nuclear attack in the past, it will likely continue to happen in the future, and it is always possible that at least one of them could lead to a nuclear response.

Catalytic Nuclear War

During the early Cold War, strategists theorized about the possibility of "catalytic nuclear war." They imagined that the United States could be attacked with nuclear weapons, and that U.S. leaders would assume, quite reasonably, that the Soviet Union had been responsible for the attack and decide to strike back. Both states would have been vastly weakened after absorbing the nuclear exchange, but what it if had not been the Soviets, but the Chinese who had initially attacked the United States? In the aftermath, the Chinese could emerge as the preeminent power. One party initiates the attack, but the attack is attributed to another party and the secret attacking state comes out of the conflict more powerful than the two victim-states.[24] Given today's more advanced intelligence, surveillance, and reconnaissance capabilities, a secret attack scenario may seem less plausible, but it is at least imaginable that a third party could begin a crisis that would bring other states to nuclear conflict.

Nuclear Use Against a Non-nuclear Opponent

In an ongoing crisis or conflict with a non-nuclear state, a nuclear-capable state may be tempted to use nuclear weapons. Nuclear use could be attractive in this situation because there would be no danger of nuclear retaliation from the targeted state, although such use

23. David Hoffman, "Cold-War Doctrines Refuse to Die," *Washington Post*, March 15, 1998, A01.

24. Donald H. Kobe, "A Theory of Catalytic War," *The Journal of Conflict Resolution* 6, No. 2 (June 1962): 125-142.

could have other ill effects, including international opprobrium.

The only case of nuclear use, against Japan during World War II, illustrates this type of use. Nuclear attacks against non-nuclear states have also been considered on at least a few other occasions. Reportedly, the French briefly contemplated nuclear use against the Vietnamese in the 1954 Battle of Dien Bien Phu during the First Indochina War.[25] Almost two decades later in the same country, U.S. President Richard Nixon mentioned the possibility of using a nuclear weapon to U.S. National Security Advisor Henry Kissinger, saying, "I'd rather use the nuclear bomb." Kissinger responded that nuclear use would be "too much" to which Nixon responded, "The nuclear bomb. Does that bother you?" He went on to say, "I just want you to think big."[26]

Thus far leaders from nuclear-capable states have appeared to agree with Kissinger that nuclear use against non-nuclear weapons states is "too much." But two points are important to note. First, the conflicts in which nuclear states have forgone nuclear use against non-nuclear states—in addition to the above conflicts, one could add China in the Korean War, the Falklands War, and the first and second Gulf Wars—were not existential threats to the nuclear states. In future conflicts with greater stakes, nuclear weapons states may be more likely to consider nuclear use. Second, there is also the possibility of nuclear use against a non-nuclear state brandishing chemical and biological weapons. The unique physical and psychological damage caused by these unconventional weapons have caused leaders to consider nuclear weapons as a potentially appropriate response and a stronger means of deterrence than conventional threats. During the 1991 Gulf War, the administration of U.S.

---

25. John Newhouse, *War and Peace in the Nuclear Age* (New York: Alfred A. Knopf, 1988), 99-101; and Martin Windrow, *The Last Valley: Dien Bien Phu and the French Defeat in Vietnam* (Cambridge, MA: Da Capo Press, 2004).

26. "Nixon Proposed Using A-Bomb in Vietnam War," *New York Times*, March 1, 2002, available from *www.nytimes.com/2002/03/01/world/nixon-proposed-using-a-bomb-in-vietnam-war.html*.

President George H.W. Bush attempted to threaten nuclear use to deter Iraqi President Saddam Hussein from using chemical weapons against U.S. soldiers.[27] Similarly, during the 2003 Iraq War, officials from the George W. Bush administration again made veiled threats of nuclear use by claiming no options were off the table to deter Iraqi use of chemical and biological weapons (CBW).[28] Bush administration officials later said they would not have used nuclear weapons, but they must have thought use was credible enough to issue the threat.

Today U.S. nuclear doctrine continues to leave open the possibility of nuclear use in response to unconventional attacks. The 2010 Nuclear Posture Review (NPR) states, "there remains a narrow range of contingencies in which U.S. nuclear weapons may still play a role in deterring a conventional or CBW attack against the United States or its allies and partners."[29] Similarly, the 2010 Russian nuclear doctrine reserves the option "to utilize nuclear weapons in response to the utilization of nuclear and other types of weapons of mass destruction against it and (or) its allies."[30]

Finally, there are those who argue that nuclear weapons should be considered in cases of cyber-attack. In January 2013, DoD's Defense Science Board issued a report arguing the United States should be prepared to use nuclear weapons in response to major cyber-attacks and Washington has not yet ruled out any such use in

27. Scott D. Sagan, "Realist Perspectives on Ethical Norms and Weapons of Mass Destruction," in Sohail H. Hashmi and Steven P. Lee, eds., *Ethics and Weapons of Mass Destruction* (Cambridge: Cambridge University Press, 2004), 81.

28. Wade Boese, "U.S. Issued Warning on Threat of Possible Iraqi WMD Use," *Arms Control Today* 33, No. 4 (May 2003).

29. Department of Defense, *Nuclear Posture Review Report* (Washington, DC: April 2010), viii.

30. "The Military Doctrine of the Russian Federation" approved by Russian Federation presidential edict on February 5, 2010, translated text available from *carnegieendowment.org/files/2010russia_military_doctrine.pdf*.

official doctrine.[31]

Splendid First Strike

A sixth potential use of nuclear weapons is the so-called "splendid first strike." The purpose of this type of nuclear use is to destroy all of an adversary's nuclear weapons in a single nuclear campaign, leaving the adversary unable to strike back with nuclear weapons.

No state has ever attempted a nuclear first strike, but such strikes have been considered. In the early Cold War it was plausible for the United States, with its head start in the nuclear arms race, to consider a splendid first strike against the Soviet Union. In April 1950, the U.S. National Security Council rejected preventive war on the nascent Soviet arsenal "on strategic and moral grounds."[32] Although the decision document, NSC-68, did allow for a pre-emptive strike if the United States were under imminent attack from the Soviet Union.[33] During the administration of U.S. President Dwight Eisenhower, military planners explored a preventive war option, with a Joint Chiefs of Staff Advance Study Group recommending the United States consider starting a war with the Soviets before their nuclear forces became "a real menace."[34] Other military leaders disagreed, in effect calling such an attack un-American, and this option was ruled out by December 1954.[35] Both the United States and the Soviets considered a nuclear first strike against China in

---

31. Defense Science Board, *Resilient Military Systems and the Advanced Cyber Threat* (Washington, DC: U.S. Department of Defense, January 2013), available from *www.acq.osd.mil/dsb/reports/ResilientMilitarySystems.CyberThreat.pdf.*

32. Scott D. Sagan, *Moving Targets: Nuclear Strategy and National Security* (Princeton, NJ: Princeton University Press, 1989), 19-20.

33. Quoted in Ibid, 20.

34. Quoted in Ibid, 21.

35. Ibid, 21-22.

the 1960s.[36]

As the Soviet Union's nuclear arsenal developed over time, Washington began to worry that its nuclear forces might themselves be vulnerable to a splendid first strike. RAND Corporation analyst Albert Wohlstetter argued that the balance of terror might be more "delicate" than previously believed and, as a result, the U.S. military dispersed its air bases and took other measures to ensure nuclear survivability.[37]

Carrying out a nuclear first strike would entail great risk. If the strike failed to destroy every single nuclear weapon of the adversary, then the attacker would risk devastating nuclear retaliation in response. Even Herman Kahn, author of On Thermonuclear War, argued that "for...practical reasons alone, not to speak of vitally important moral and political ones, the notion of having a Splendid First Strike Capability seems fanciful."[38] This type of nuclear use would be most plausible, therefore, against a target state that possessed relatively few weapons at known locations.

Though there are no historical examples of a splendid first strike using nuclear weapons, the strategic logic underpinning this type of attack, to wipe out an adversary's nuclear capability in one strike

---

36. On Soviet interest in attacking Chinese nuclear facilities see, U.S. State Department Memorandum of Conversation, "US Reaction to Soviet Destruction of CPR [Chinese Peoples Republic] Nuclear Capability; Significance of Latest Sino-Soviet Border Clash, ...," August 18, 1969, Secret/Sensitive, National Archives, SN 67-69, Def 12 Chicom, available from *www2.gwu.edu/~nsarchiv/NSAEBB/NSAEBB49/sino.sov.10.pdf*. On U.S. considerations see William Burr and Jeffrey T. Richelson, "Whether to 'Strangle the Baby in the Cradle:' The United States and the Chinese Nuclear Program, 1960-64," *International Security* 25, No. 3 (Winter 2000-01): 54-99.

37. Albert Wohlstetter, "The Delicate Balance of Terror," RAND Report P-1472, November 6, 1958. Available from *www.rand.org/about/history/wohlstetter/P1472/P1472.html*.

38. Herman Kahn, *On Thermonuclear War* (Princeton NJ: Princeton University Press, 1960), 37.

to prevent one's own state from being targeted in the future, has been pursued by states using conventional weapons. In destroying Iraq's Osirak nuclear reactor in 1981, for example, Israel attempted to take out Iraq's developing nuclear capability, striking before it had a more developed weapons program. Israel took similar action when bombing the Syrian al-Kibar reactor in September 2007. If a country were further along in a nuclear weapons program and conventional weapons were insufficient to destroy an enemy nuclear program, it is conceivable that leaders would consider nuclear weapons appropriate for the task for the same underlying reasons.

Use 'Em or Lose 'Em

In a crisis situation involving two nuclear-armed states, each may fear their nuclear weapons will be vulnerable to attack by their adversary and thus decide to use them before they are wiped out. Pressure to "use 'em or lose 'em" in a crisis might be heightened if a country possesses a nuclear arsenal that is vulnerable to a splendid first strike or if the adversary's nuclear posture favors the offense. For example, during the Cold War, each side maintained ballistic missiles with relatively accurate multiple independently targetable reentry vehicles (MIRVs). With this capability, a single missile could target and destroy a number of the adversary's nuclear weapons. Even if all of the targeted state's missiles were not destroyed, it would be left at great numerical disadvantage vis-à-vis the attacking state. This condition meant each side felt immense pressure to launch its missiles first in the event of conflict, leading to the development of "launch on warning" postures in which weapons already on alert could be quickly deployed if an incoming attack were detected. In this situation, it might be more reasonable for a leader to simply back down rather than initiate a nuclear war from such a disadvantaged position, but it is possible that a future leader would prefer to use them than lose them.

Nuclear Brinksmanship

Many scholars and practitioners incorrectly believe that nuclear use is impossible, or at the very least irrational, once one's adversary possesses a secure second-strike capability. If an adversary has the ability to absorb a nuclear attack and respond with a devastating counterattack, then one can no longer hope to conduct a splendid first strike and any nuclear use could result in unacceptable retaliation. Meanwhile, states would not feel the same use 'em or lose 'em pressures, because they would understand that they could ride out a nuclear attack and still hit back with force. Since both sides understand these facts, a situation of restraint arises due to the condition of Mutually Assured Destruction (MAD). Yet, nuclear deterrence theorists have identified several rational uses of nuclear weapons even in a condition of MAD.

Thomas Schelling was the first to devise a rational means by which states can threaten nuclear-armed opponents.[39] He argued that leaders cannot credibly threaten to intentionally launch a suicidal nuclear war, but they can make a "threat that leaves something to chance."[40] They can engage in a process, a nuclear crisis, which increases the risk of nuclear war in an attempt to force a less resolved adversary to back down. As states escalate a nuclear crisis there is an increasing probability that the conflict will spiral out of control and result in an inadvertent or accidental nuclear exchange. As long as the benefit of winning the crisis is greater than the incremental increase in the risk of nuclear war, threats to escalate nuclear crises are inherently credible. In these games of nuclear brinkmanship, the state that is willing to run the greatest risk of nuclear war before backing down will win the crisis as long as it does not end in catastrophe. It is for this reason that Schelling called great power

---

39. Thomas Schelling, *The Strategy of Conflict* (Cambridge, MA: Harvard University Press, 1960).

40. Ibid., 127.

politics in the nuclear era a "competition in risk taking."[41]

This does not mean that states eagerly bid up the risk of nuclear war. Rather, they face gut-wrenching decisions at each stage of the crisis. They can quit the crisis to avoid nuclear war, but only by ceding an important geopolitical issue to an opponent. Or they can escalate the crisis in an attempt to prevail, but only at the risk of suffering a possible nuclear exchange.

On brinksmanship, U.S. Secretary of States John Foster Dulles stated, "The ability to get to the verge without getting into the war is the necessary art... If you try to run away from it, if you are scared to go to the brink, you are lost."[42] The bipolar Cold War conflict provides several examples of nuclear brinksmanship, with the Cuban Missile Crisis as the most notable. Soviet Premier Nikita Khrushchev initially raised the stakes by placing nuclear weapons in Cuba, gravely threatening the U.S. homeland and meddling within the U.S. sphere of influence. In response, U.S. President John F. Kennedy escalated by placing a blockade around the island so Soviet ships could not deliver additional missiles. In the end, the Soviet Union withdrew its missiles from Cuba, but not before the risk of nuclear war was raised to, in President Kennedy's mind, "between 1 in 3 and even."[43]

Other historical examples of brinkmanship include Moscow's threats against the British and the French during the 1956 Suez Crisis, Moscow's threats to attack China during the Sino-Soviet border war in 1969, President Nixon's nuclear alerts in 1969 and 1973, and finally, Indian and Pakistani threats and nuclear weapons

---

41. Thomas Schelling, *Arms and Influence* (New Haven, CT: Yale University Press, 1966), 91.

42. John Lamberton Harper, *The Cold War* (Oxford: Oxford University Press, 2011), 117-118.

43. Quoted in Graham Allison, "The Cuban Missile Crisis at 50: Lessons for U.S. Foreign Policy Today," *Foreign Affairs* 91, No. 4 (July/August 2012): 11-16.

movements during the 1999 Kargil Crisis.[44] Looking to the future, as long as rivalries continue and as long as leaders are willing to initiate and escalate high stakes crises in search of their geopolitical goals, the risk of war through nuclear brinkmanship will remain with us.

Limited Nuclear War

During the course of the Cold War nuclear strategists considered an alternative to all-out nuclear war between the two superpowers: limited nuclear war.[45] This is conflict "in which each side exercises restraint in the use of nuclear weapons, employing only a limited number of weapons on selected targets."[46] By launching a single nuclear weapon against a small city or an isolated military base, for example, a nuclear-armed state could signal its willingness to escalate a crisis, while leaving its adversary with enough left to lose to deter the adversary from launching a full-scale nuclear response. U.S. proponents of limited nuclear war included Henry Kissinger and Robert Osgood.[47] In his 1957 book Nuclear Weapons and Foreign Policy, Kissinger argued that the United States should be prepared for alternatives to "all-out" nuclear war, especially in peripheral conflicts.[48] Limited nuclear war, he argues, cannot be "improvised" during the course of conflict, but it has "its own ap-

---

44. Kroenig, "Nuclear Superiority and the Balance of Resolve," (2013): 141-171.

45. Klaus Knorr, *Limited Strategic War* (New York: Praeger, 1962).

46. Jeff A. Larsen, and James M. Smith, *Historical Dictionary of Arms Control and Disarmament* (Lanham, MD: Scarecrow Press, 2005), 128.

47. Morton H. Halperin provides a helpful summary of the debate over limited nuclear in the 1950s in "Nuclear Weapons and Limited War," T*he Journal of Conflict Resolution* 5, No. 2 (June 1961): 146-166.

48. Henry A. Kissinger, *Nuclear Weapons and Foreign Policy* (New York, NY: Council on Foreign Relations, 1957): 177.

propriate tactics…with limitations as to targets, areas and the size of weapons used."[49] Most importantly, limited nuclear war requires communicating to adversaries in advance the understandings of limited war, otherwise "miscalculations and misinterpretations" of intentions "may cause the war to become all-out even if both sides intend to limit it."[50]

In the current era there are a number of conflicts in which adversaries could engage in limited nuclear war. Because arsenal sizes vary, the defining feature of this type of nuclear war is not that it seeks to avoid all-out nuclear exchange, but that nuclear weapons are employed with some level of restraint, to avoid the widespread use of nuclear weapons on both sides.

History provides examples of states planning to deploy nuclear weapons in a limited way to achieve limited aims. During the early Cold War when the United States was conventionally inferior to the Soviet Union, U.S. leaders felt they had no choice but to go nuclear to stop Soviets from overrunning Europe. This is similar to France's approach to nuclear strategy during the Cold War. Vastly overmatched by Moscow, the French plan was also to resort to launching nuclear weapons as soon as conventional fighting began.[51] Similarly, at present, America's conventionally inferior adversaries have incentives to use nuclear weapons early in a crisis in an attempt to deter further escalation and ensure their own survival.[52]

---

49. Ibid, 185.

50. Ibid.

51. For a thorough discussion of the development of French nuclear strategy, see Bruno Tertais, "Destruction Assuree: The Origins and Development of French Nuclear Strategy, 1945-1982," in Henry D. Sokolski ed., *Getting MAD: Nuclear Mutual Assured Destruction, Its Origins and Practice* (Carlisle, PA: Strategic Studies Institute, 2004), 64.

52. Keir A. Lieber and Daryl G. Press, "The Nukes We Need," *Foreign Affairs* 88, No. 6 (November/December 2009): 42.

Identifying the Next Nuclear War

Having reviewed the various pathways that could produce nuclear war in theory, we turn to the empirics to examine the countries with the capabilities and political conflicts that could conceivably produce the next nuclear war. Nine states currently possess nuclear weapons, and a tenth, Iran, appears to be seeking at least a latent nuclear capability. Although nuclear use by any one state appears unlikely, there are a number of potential conflicts involving nuclear-armed states that could lead to nuclear use. In addition to states, a handful of terrorist organizations have expressed desire to employ nuclear weapons. The following section examines the nuclear capabilities and doctrines of these actors and the geopolitical conflicts that could escalate into nuclear use in the future. Indeed, certain trends in nuclear force modernization, doctrine, and regional enmities suggest nuclear use may have become more, not less, likely in recent years.

Russia, the United States, and NATO

Under the New Strategic Arms Reduction Treaty (New START), the United States and Russia agreed to limit their arsenals to 1,550 deployed nuclear warheads and 800 total delivery platforms by 2018. The United States maintains a nuclear triad, with nuclear warheads delivered by intercontinental ballistic missiles (ICBMs), submarine launched ballistic missiles (SLBMs), and bomber aircraft, and is in the early planning stages for modernizing each of these platforms. In the 2010 Nuclear Posture Review, Washington vowed not to use or threaten to use nuclear weapons against non-nuclear states in good standing with the Nuclear Nonproliferation Treaty (NPT) and their nonproliferation commitments.[53] For states not covered by this negative security assurance, U.S. leaders may consider nuclear weapons for deterring nuclear, conventional, biological, or even cyber-attacks. The report concludes that the United

---

53. *Nuclear Posture Review Report*, 15.

States "would only consider the use of nuclear weapons in extreme circumstances to defend the vital interests of the United States or its allies and partners."[54]

Russia also maintains a nuclear triad, including ICBMs (some of which are road-mobile), SLBMs, and bombers and it is modernizing all of its delivery systems. Russia is in the process of equipping more of its ICBMs with MIRVs, a move that many consider destabilizing, especially in relation to the de-MIRVed U.S. ICBM force.[55] In addition, Russia is working on new ICBMs, including a heavy ICBM with as many as ten warheads to replace the retiring SS-18.[56] Russia is reportedly developing a new rail-mobile system, the "Barguzin" that will allow it to very quickly move nuclear weapons around its vast territory.[57] Russia is also developing a new stealth, long-range bomber with production to begin in 2020. Moscow is also modernizing the sea leg with plans for eight new Borei-class submarines armed with 16 Bulava missiles, containing six warheads each.[58] In addition to the strategic force, Russia is estimated to maintain between 1,000 and 6,000 tactical or nonstrategic weapons in its arsenal.[59]

Unlike the United States, which has sought to reduce its reliance on nuclear weapons since the end of the Cold War, Russia has developed a greater role for these weapons in the past decade. This change has stemmed primarily from an imbalance in conventional

---

54. Ibid., 17.

55. Hans M. Kristensen and Robert S. Norris, "Russian Nuclear Forces 2014," Bulletin of the Atomic Scientists, Vol. 70, No. 2, March/April 2014, pp. 75-85.

56 . Ibid., 78.

57. Ben Hoyle, 'Russia's Cold War nuclear missile train back on track in new arms race," *The Australian*, December 2, 2014.

58. Ibid., 79.

59. Amy F. Woolf, "Nonstrategic Nuclear Weapons," RL32572, (Washington, DC: Congressional Research Service, January 3, 2014).

capabilities vis-à-vis the United States. In the post-Cold War period, Russia's conventional forces have been vastly inferior to Western capabilities and they lowered their doctrinal threshold for nuclear use in an attempt to offset this weakness. In the 1990s, Russia stated that the sole purpose of nuclear weapons was deterrence of large-scale attacks that threaten the state existentially, but by 2000, Russia reserved "the right to use nuclear weapons in response to the use of nuclear and other types of weapons of mass destruction against it and (or) its allies, as well as in response to large-scale aggression utilizing conventional weapons in situations critical to the national security of the Russian Federation."[60] The 2010 doctrine moderated this statement somewhat, but it is clear that nuclear weapons remain central to Russian strategy as military thinkers in Russia argue that in the course of a large conventional conflict nuclear weapons could be utilized as means of "de-escalation." Moreover, since 1999, nuclear weapons have featured prominently in Russian military exercises and in March 2014, Russia performed a large-scale nuclear exercise that was presided over by Russian President Vladimir Putin himself.[61] Russian leaders engaged in outright nuclear saber-rattling over the crisis in Ukraine, beginning in 2014 and even threatened Denmark that it would become a target of Russian nuclear missiles if it hosted part of NATO's missile defense system.[62]

As the successor state of the Soviet Union, Russia has a long history of conflict with the United States and the countries of the North

---

60. "Военная Доктрина Российской Федерации" (Russia's Military Doctrine), Утверждена Указом Президента Российской Федерации от 21 апреля 2000 г. N 706 (Approved by Presidential Decree on 21 April, 2000 N. 706), available from *www.rg.ru/oficial/doc/ykazi/doc_war.htm*. An English translation of the doctrine is available from *www.armscontrol.org/act/2000_05/dc3ma00*.

61. Ibid., x.; Zachary Keck, "Russia's Military Begins Massive Nuclear War Drill," *The Diplomat*, March 29, 2014; and "U.S. Conducts Nuclear Response Exercises," *Global Security Newswire*, May 12, 2014.

62. David M. Herszenhorn, "Russian Warns Denmark on Joining NATO Missile Defense," *The New York Times*, March 22, 2015.

Atlantic Treaty Organization (NATO). For forty years these two powers teetered on the brink of nuclear war, especially during periods of high tension, including the Korean War, the 1956 Suez Crisis, the 1961 Berlin Crisis, and the 1962 Cuban Missile Crisis. Though the ideological struggle between the United States and the Soviet Union ended with the dissolution of the Soviet Union in 1991, tensions between these two states remain. Nationalism has grown in recent years with Russian strongman Vladimir Putin declaring in 2005 that the dissolution of the Soviet Union was the "greatest geopolitical catastrophe" of the twentieth century.[63] As of this writing, reports indicate Russia maintains thousands of troops inside eastern Ukraine, with thousands more on the border. NATO is planning a number of military exercises with allies on the Russian periphery including a March 2015 exercise in the Black Sea with Romania and upcoming military drills with Bulgaria.[64]

Indeed, the most likely flashpoint for U.S./NATO and Russian conflict today is in Russia's periphery. In 2008, Russia invaded its neighbor Georgia and the current crisis over Ukraine highlights the persistent tension between Russia and the West over NATO expansion and what Russia perceives as encroachment in its traditional sphere of influence. In addition to Georgia and Ukraine, one can imagine future conflict between Russia and NATO members such as Estonia, Latvia, Lithuania, and Poland, where Russia retains historical and cultural interest and may find reason for interference. If Russia were to use force against a NATO country, Washington would be obligated by the NATO charter to come to its ally's defense. And a Russian and NATO conflict in Europe would take place under the shadow of nuclear war.

---

63. Andrew Osborn, "Putin: Collapse of the Soviet Union was 'catastrophe of the century,'" *The Independent* (London), April 26, 2005.

64. See, for example, "6 ships arrive in Black Sea to take part in NATO exercises," *The Associated Press*, March 13, 2015; and "Bulgaria, United States to begin military drills amid Ukraine Crisis," *Reuters*, March 13, 2015.

China and the United States

Chinese military capabilities, including its nuclear arsenal, are smaller and less effective than those of the United States, but China is in the midst of a three-decade process of translating its economic prowess into vast military power. By some calculations its military budget is now almost $200 billion, second only to the United States.[65] The Chinese have traditionally been comfortable with a nuclear posture that has been described as a minimal deterrent, but the People's Liberation Army's (PLA) 2005 Science of Military Strategy planning calls for the development of a "lean and effective" arsenal, with many Western analysts noting that the emphasis is on the "effective."[66] Current estimates indicate China has approximately 250 warheads in its stockpile and this number is expected to expand.[67] Approximately 60 of these weapons are on missiles capable of reaching the continental United States.[68] The 2013 DoD report to Congress on Chinese military capabilities recounts continued Chinese investments in ballistic missiles, cruise missiles, counter-space weapons, and "military cyberspace capabilities that appear designed to enable anti-access/area-denial (A2/AD) missions."[69] The PLA Rocket Force, in control of Chinese conventional and nuclear ballistic missiles, in recent years has added two types of road-mobile ballistic missiles to its arsenal and one of these modifications can reach most locations in the United States. The DoD report speculates the PLA Rocket Force may be developing a MIRV capability for a new road-mobile ICBM.

---

65. Zachary Keck, "China's Defense Budget: A Mixed Bag," *The Diplomat*, March 8, 2014.

66. Peng Guangqian & Yao Youzhi, eds., *Science of Military Strategy* (Beijing: Military Science Publishing House, 2005).

67. Hans M. Kristensen and Robert S. Norris, "Chinese nuclear forces, 2013," *Bulletin of the Atomic Scientists* 69, No. 6 (November/December 2013): 79.

68. Ibid.

69. Office of the Secretary of Defense, "Annual Report to Congress: Military and Security Developments Involving the People's Republic of China 2013," i.

MIRVs, maneuverable reentry vehicles (MaRVs), anti-satellite capabilities, and penetration aids are all being developed to overcome U.S. ballistic missile defenses.[70] In addition, China has built an "underground great wall," a 3,000 mile tunnel network in which to house and protect its mobile nuclear missiles. The Chinese Navy is developing a sea-based nuclear deterrent, with three Jin-class submarines in testing and as many as five in development. These submarines will eventually carry SLBMs. The Chinese also have bombers capable of delivering nuclear weapons.

If a crisis in the region were to grow into a larger conflict, what does Chinese nuclear doctrine suggest about its willingness to use nuclear weapons? Since detonating its first nuclear weapon in 1964, China has persistently claimed to follow a "no first use policy," although its doctrine carves out space for exceptions. For example, the 2005 Science of Military Strategy document declared that China would only use nuclear weapons in response to a strategic attack, but that a strategic attack would not necessarily involve nuclear weapons and could even be political or psychological in nature.[71] Moreover, China's conventional inferiority when faced with an adversary like the United States may cause its leaders to consider escalation to nuclear weapons in a future conflict short of a "strategic attack," just like many of the conventionally inferior nuclear-capable states discussed above. For the first time, China's 2013 White Paper did not explicitly state China's "no first use policy" leading some to speculate that concern with U.S. conventional capabilities may merit the option of using nuclear weapons first.[72]

In the past, Taiwan has been the assumed flashpoint for potential U.S.-China conflict.[73] The United States maintains a commitment

70. Ibid, 31.

71. Peng & Yao, eds., *Science of Military Strategy*, 2005.

72. James Acton, "Is China Changing Its Position on Nuclear Weapons?' *New York Times*, April 18, 2013.

73. See for example, Kenneth Lieberthal, "Preventing a War Over Taiwan,"

 Should We Let the Bomb Spread

to support Taiwan through the Taiwan Relations Act of 1979 and has sold Taiwan advanced weaponry. Meanwhile, China's military modernization has focused on regional contingencies, including a Taiwan scenario. The U.S. and China engaged in an intense crisis over the island in 1995 and 1996 when the Chinese government test fired missiles near Taiwan in reaction to political developments on the island and a Taiwanese presidential visit to the United States. U.S. President Bill Clinton responded by sending two carrier battle groups to the South China Sea in a visible show of American military support for Taiwan. Relations between China and Taiwan have improved since 2008, but elections in 2016 brought a more nationalistic government to power in Taiwan and renewed tensions.

More recently, other regional disputes have taken center stage as China's growing power has led it to assert a sphere of influence that overlaps with areas claimed by U.S. allies and partners, as well as seas in which the U.S. Navy has long sailed uncontested. China has ongoing disputes with Japan over the Diaoyu/Senkaku islands in the East China Sea and with Vietnam, Indonesia, Malaysia, and the Philippines over islands in the South China Sea. The geography of the region creates many opportunities for miscalculation. Chinese naval ships pass within sight of Japan when heading to the Pacific Ocean. Fishing and shipping vessels regularly end up in disputed territory. Seemingly small incidents at sea could lead to crisis, which if not managed well, could lead to broader conflict. In May of 2014, Japan reported that two Chinese fighter jets had flown dangerously close to its reconnaissance planes in two separate incidents in airspace both states claim. China appears to be literally testing the waters (and the skies) to illustrate its growing strength in the region, behavior that has high risk of resulting in a clash.

Recent Chinese military exercises also demonstrate that Beijing is preparing for hostilities beyond a Taiwan scenario. In MISSION ACTION 2013, Chinese forces simulated an invasion of the Senkaku islands. After tracking the exercise, the chief of intelligence of the U.S. Pacific Fleet stated, "[We] concluded that the PLA has been given the new task to be able to conduct a short sharp war to destroy Japanese forces in the East China Sea following with what can only be expected a seizure of the Senkakus or even a southern Ryukyu [islands]."[74] Chinese exercises also demonstrate China's desire to break out of its geographic confines and become a blue water naval power. In a winter 2013 exercise called MANEU-VER 5, Chinese forces successfully fought through the "first island chain" into the Pacific Ocean.[75]

Unlike the U.S.-Soviet relationship, the United States and China do not enjoy a history of interaction that promotes stability. Each side may only be able to learn lessons about the other's crisis signaling, redlines, and crisis communications only through dangerous experience. For example, the United States and China do not have a Cold War-style hotline set up between their highest leadership to mitigate the risk that misperceptions could lead to war (a line between the DoD and Chinese Defense Ministry has not yet been tested in a period of tension). China is notable for its lack of transparency, especially in the nuclear realm. This position is understandable for a power which maintains fewer nuclear weapons than potential adversaries, but it does mean misunderstandings or miscalculations might be even more likely.

Russia and China

A final great power dyad in which nuclear war is possible is Russia and China. Both have large and sophisticated nuclear arsenals, although, as described above, Russia maintains a clear nuclear superiority. But China's conventional and nuclear capabilities are grow-

---

74. Sam LaGrone, "Navy Official: China Training for 'Short Sharp War' with Japan" *USNI News*, February 18, 2014.

75. Andrew Berglund, "'Maneuver-5' Exercise Focuses on Improving Distant Seas Combat Capabilities," *U.S.-China Economic and Security Review Commission Staff Report*, December 16, 2013.

ing and its two million-member army is of concern to Moscow.

The two powers have clashed over their 2,700-mile border through-out the decades and in 1969, during the Sino-Soviet Border War, the Soviet Union issued explicit nuclear threats against China. In the 1990s and 2000s, the countries agreed to officially end the bor-der disputes and there have even been subsequent signs of coopera-tion. Yet, despite some shared interests due in part to a shared per-ception of threat from Washington and its allies, Russia is watching China's rise and military modernization warily. Indeed, Moscow is changing its nuclear posture in response to developments in Bei-jing. Over the past several years, Moscow has been cheating on the 1987 Intermediate Nuclear Forces (INF) Treaty by developing a land-based nuclear missile in the banned 300-3,400 mile range and Russian officials are quite clear that the nuclear forces are a neces-sary response to Chinese intermediate range nuclear forces. While it is hard to conceive of a direct military struggle between these two powers in the near term, the rise of China will continue to pose an increasing threat to Russia. It is likely that relations between these two great powers will ebb and flow over time, and if and when they worsen to the point of another direct military confrontation, nuclear weapons will be present.

North Korea, South Korea, Japan, and the United States

Over the past decade, the Democratic People's Republic of Korea (DPRK) has demonstrated its growing nuclear and missile capa-bilities. It is currently estimated to possess enough fissile material for between thirteen and thirty nuclear warheads.[76] It is unclear, however, whether Pyongyang has yet developed the capability to miniaturize weapons for delivery on missiles. North Korea has developed short and medium-range weapons that can reach South

---

76. David Albright and Christina Walrond, "North Korea's Estimated Stocks of Plutonium and Weapon-Grade Uranium," *Institute for Science and International Security*, August 16, 2012.

Korea and Japan, but has not yet successfully test launched an in-
tercontinental-range missile.

Relations between Pyongyang and its neighbors are openly hostile.
North and South Korea have technically been in an armistice since
1953 when fighting in the Korean War ended. Both states claim the
right to the entire peninsula and they have had tense relations since
the end of the war that have occasionally included direct military
attacks. At present, Japan and North Korea do not maintain official
diplomatic relations. They also have a long history of ill-will stem-
ming from the Japanese occupation of Korea in the early part of the
twentieth century and the kidnapping of Japanese citizens by North
Korea in the 1970s and 1980s.

In recent years, Pyongyang has taken provocative action against
both South Korea and Japan, such as shelling South Korea's Yeon-
pyeong Island in 2010, sinking a South Korean warship in 2010,
and test-firing missiles into the Sea of Japan. In January 2014,
DPRK leadership threatened nuclear war in the run up to Republic of Korea (ROK)-U.S. military exercises, complaining that these
joint exercises are preparation for an invasion of North Korea.[77]

The situation in North Korea is especially volatile because Kim
Jung-Un has already demonstrated willingness to take drastic action to solidify his position and remain in power and due to similar domestic pressures he may have incentives to create a crisis in
which nuclear use becomes possible.

If North Korea's erratic behavior continues or escalates, there is
a potential for the United States to become involved in a conflict
based on its treaty commitments to South Korea and Japan. Since
they face nuclear adversaries, U.S. reassurance tends to include a
heavy emphasis on nuclear capabilities. In the spring of 2013, for
example, the U.S. flew two nuclear-capable B-2s over the Peninsula to threaten the North and reassure the South.

---

77. "North Korea threatens nuclear war in run-up to US-South Korea war
games," *Associated Press*, January 29, 2014.

North Korea does not publicize an official nuclear doctrine, although its rhetoric has been bellicose and has included explicit nuclear threats against the United States and South Korea in the recent past. If Kim Jung Un enters into an open conflict with the vastly superior United States, he may have incentive to use nuclear weapons in an attempt to bring a rapid halt to the conflict and to preserve his life and his regime. With such a small and vulnerable arsenal, Kim might also feel "use 'em or lose 'em" pressure, encouraging him to go nuclear early in a conflict. If Pyongyang were to use nuclear weapons, some analysts assume DPRK would employ a countervalue strategy, aiming its weapons at cities in neighboring South Korea or Japan.

If U.S. reassurances prove insufficient, it is always possible that Japan or South Korea could decide to build independent nuclear deterrent forces. Japan has considered and then rejected nuclear weapons three times in the nuclear age and to this day possesses what is essentially a latent nuclear weapons capability. Due to its well-known "nuclear allergy," nuclear proliferation in Japan seems unlikely in the near-term, but it remains possible. In South Korea, recent polling indicates that two-thirds of citizens support developing nuclear weapons.[78] South Korea has also been actively seeking indigenous reprocessing technology for peaceful purposes, but that could help Seoul develop a weapons capability at some point in the future. If Japan and South Korea join the United States, China, and North Korea as nuclear powers, East Asia would become a poly-nuclear region, rife with geopolitical tensions and rivalries that would be ripe for the next nuclear conflict.

India and Pakistan

If asked where a nuclear exchange is most likely today, many analysts would select the Indian subcontinent. The longstanding rivalry

---

78. Martin Fackler and Choe Sang-Hun, "South Korea Flirts With Nuclear Ideas as North Blusters," *New York Times*, March 10, 2013.

between these two nuclear-capable states has involved numerous crises. They have an on-going territorial dispute over Kashmir, an active arms race, and the instability generated by a conventionally inferior and revisionist Pakistan armed with nuclear weapons.

The two nuclear powers are currently engaged in a nuclear arms race. Pakistan has the world's fastest growing nuclear arsenal.[79] Currently it is estimated to have 110 weapons, while making enough highly enriched uranium for 10-15 weapons per year.[80] In addition, Pakistan has a growing plutonium production capability, with China agreeing to provide as many as three new reactors.[81] Its delivery vehicles include aircraft and surface-to-surface missiles.[82] Pakistan recently added a maneuverable, short-range, sub-kiloton battlefield nuclear missile to its arsenal, the Hatf IX or Nasr, allowing it to quickly use nuclear weapons against an advancing Indian army (and just as worrisome, the mobility of these missiles raises concerns about secure military custody of the weapons).[83] Pakistan does not publish a formal nuclear doctrine, though its leaders have declared that its nuclear weapons exist to deter India.

India has approximately 100 warheads in its arsenal and is in the process of developing a nuclear triad. India possesses nuclear-capable aircraft, nuclear-capable missiles that cover both short and long ranges, and is currently developing ICBMs as well as submarine-launched missiles. India has a long-held policy of the "no first use"

---

79. Hans M. Kristensen and Robert S. Norris, "Pakistan's nuclear forces, 2011," *Bulletin of the Atomic Scientists* 67, No. 4 (July/August 2011).

80. Nuclear Threat Initiative, "Pakistan-Country Profiles," December 2014, available from *www.nti.org/country-profiles/pakistan/nuclear/*.

81. Saeed Shah, "Pakistan in Talks to Acquire 3 Nuclear Plants From China," *Wall Street Journal*, January 20, 2014.

82. Paul K. Kerr and Mary Beth Nikitin, "Pakistan's Nuclear Weapons: Proliferation and Security Issues," *CRS Report for Congress*, February 13, 2013.

83. Usman Ansari, "Experts: Missile Test Firing Shows Development Complete," *Defense News*, November 6, 2013.

of nuclear weapons. The party of Indian Prime Minister Narendra Modi has vowed to "revise and update" India's nuclear doctrine writing that "the strategic gains acquired by India during the Atal Bihari Vajpayee regime on the nuclear programme have been frittered away by the Congress."[84] Thus it is possible that the doctrine will be altered both in response to Pakistan's nuclear development and recent changes in China's doctrine.

The two states have been in conflict since their founding and violent partition in 1948. They fought wars in 1965 over Kashmir and in 1971 when East Pakistan became the independent state of Bangladesh. In May 1998, India conducted five nuclear tests and within weeks Pakistan responded with six tests of its own. The most dangerous period in the nuclear era occurred a year later in 1999 when Pakistani forces crossed the Line of Control in Kashmir and occupied part of the Kargil district, resulting in an Indian counterattack and worldwide fears of nuclear war. A 2001 terrorist attack on the Indian parliament in New Delhi and another terrorist attack in Mumbai in 2008 also flamed tension between the nuclear adversaries and raised the specter of nuclear conflict.

A terrorist attack or small conflict on the border between the two states could quickly escalate to the nuclear level. In 2004 India developed the "Cold Start" military doctrine, a plan to mobilize conventional forces on the Pakistani border within 48 hours of receiving orders. The goal of the plan is to quickly overwhelm Pakistan with limited territorial aims before international actors can intervene. Because of its conventional inferiority, however, analysts assume Pakistan would resort to nuclear weapons early in a large-scale conventional war. Its recent development of battlefield nuclear weapons indicates a lowering of the threshold for nuclear use. Indeed, former Pakistani Ambassador to the United States Maleeha Lodhi has argued that Pakistan needed to develop these tactical weapons "to counterbalance India's move to bring conventional

---

84. The 2014 "Election Manifesto" of the BJP is available from, *www.bjp.org/images/pdf_2014/full_manifesto_english_07.04.2014.pdf.*

military offensives to a tactical level," suggesting these weapons are to be deployed against advancing Indian troops. Once nuclear weapons are used, however, even if only tactical, it might be difficult to control the escalation.

Iran, Israel, and the United States

Israel is estimated to possess approximately 75 to 200 nuclear weapons.[85] It has advanced missile capabilities with its Jericho ballistic missile, nuclear-capable aircraft, and may deploy cruise missiles with nuclear warheads on its Dolphin-class submarines, possibly providing it with a second strike capability.[86] Because of its policy of nuclear opacity (animut) and promise not "to be the first country to introduce nuclear weapons in the Middle East,"[87] we know little about Israel's nuclear doctrine.

Iran's nuclear program is at least temporarily halted under the Joint Comprehensive Plan of Action struck with the international community in 2015. But if the limits in this deal were contravened for any reason, it is possible that Iran could still join the nuclear club. If Iran acquires nuclear weapons, it is also possible that other states in the region, including Turkey, Egypt, or Saudi Arabia could attempt to acquire nuclear weapons in response.[88] While fears of a rapid and

---

85. The Arms Control Association provides this range. See "Nuclear Weapons: Who Has What at a Glance," *Arm Control Association*, June 13, 2014. The Federation of American Scientists put the estimate at 80 weapons. "Status of World Nuclear Forces," *Federation of American Scientists*, April 30, 2014.

86. Peter Beaumont and Conal Urquhart, "Israel deploys nuclear arms in submarines," The Guardian, October 11, 2003, available from *https://www.theguardian.com/world/2003/oct/12/israel1*.

87. Robert S. Norris, William M. Arkin, Hans M. Kristensen and Joshua Handler, "Israeli Nuclear Forces, 2002," *Bulletin of the Atomic Scientists* 58, No. 5 (September 2002): 73.

88. James M. Lindsay and Ray Takeyh, "After Iran Gets the Bomb: Containment and Its Complications," *Foreign Affairs* 89, No. 2 (March/April 2010): 33-49.

complete nuclear cascade in the region are probably overblown, it is possible, if not likely, that one or two additional states would join the nuclear club within the course of several decades if Iran goes nuclear.[89]

The nuclear balance of power between Iran and its neighbors could be highly unstable and would likely lack many of the safeguards that existed between the superpowers during the Cold War, including: the absence of a direct line of communication between Iran and its rivals, short timelines for nuclear-armed missiles to travel between states, the lack of secure second-strike capabilities (at least initially), and, in Israel, a lack of strategic depth and a strategic culture that emphasizes preemption.

Iran and Israel have viewed each other as strategic competitors since the Iranian Revolution in 1979; Israel has directly come into conflict with Iran's proxies, Hezbollah and Hamas. Iran has also frequently clashed with Israel's superpower patron, the United States. In 1988, the United States and Iran engaged in a major naval battle as part of the Tanker War, the U.S. Navy's largest engagement since the end of World War II. Iran sponsored proxy attacks that killed U.S. service personnel for a decade in Iraq and Afghanistan. And Tehran and Washington frequently exchange threats and counter-threats in the Persian Gulf and over the Strait of Hormuz.[90] It is, therefore, conceivable that a future conflict involving a nuclear-armed Iran and Israel or the United States could result in a nuclear exchange. If other states in the region, such as Turkey or Saudi Arabia, also acquired nuclear weapons, the nuclear balance would be even less stable and a poly-nuclear Middle East might be the most likely candidate for the next nuclear war.

89. Matthew Kroenig, *A Time to Attack: The Looming Iranian Nuclear Threat* (New York: Palgrave Macmillan, 2014).

90. For example, see Rick Gladstone, "Noise Level Rises Over Iran Threat to Close Strait of Hormuz," *New York Times*, December 28, 2011.

Nuclear Terrorism

Since the terrorist attacks on September 11, 2001, scholars, analysts, and politicians have focused on the nexus of nuclear weapons and terrorism. In his closing statement at the 2012 Nuclear Security Summit, U.S. President Barack Obama concluded, "We've agreed that nuclear terrorism is one of the most urgent and serious threats to global security."[91] Though there has been some debate on how seriously this threat should be taken,[92] evidence indicates that terrorist organizations have both expressed a desire for nuclear weapons and made attempts to buy or seize nuclear material. Declassified documents from the United States suggest al Qaeda leader Osama bin Laden directed his associates to purchase uranium.[93] In addition, Chechnya-based separatist groups, Lashkar-e-Taiba in South Asia, and Aum Shinrikyo in Japan have also expressed the desire for nuclear weapons in the past.[94]

Most analysts consider it unlikely that a state would knowingly provide a terrorist group with a bomb, but it is conceivable that a group could steal one. This fear is especially acute in the case of Pakistan, where an unstable government with a growing nuclear arsenal exists in an area with many terrorist organizations. The government of Pakistan has taken steps in recent years to allay these

---

91. White House, Office of the Press Secretary, "Remarks by President Obama at Opening Plenary Session of the Nuclear Security Summit," Coex Center, Seoul, Republic of Korea, March 27, 2012.

92. John Mueller is probably the most notable skeptic of the nexus between terrorists and nuclear weapons. See *Overblown: How Politicians and the Terrorism Industry Inflate National Security Threats, and Why We Believe Them* (New York: Free Press, 2006).

93. See Documents 2 and 3 in "Nuclear Terrorism: How Big a Threat? Is al-Qaeda Trying to Get a Bomb? Documents Trace U.S. Nuclear Counter-Terror Efforts," National Security Archive Electronic Briefing Book No. 388, September 2012, available from *www2.gwu.edu/~nsarchiv/nukevault/ebb388/*.

94. Graham Allison, "Nuclear Terrorism Fact Sheet," *Belfer Center for Science and International Affairs*, Harvard Kennedy School, April 2010.

fears, yet reason for concern remains.[95]

A second means by which a terrorist group could attain a nuclear capability is by obtaining fissile material and constructing its own crude nuclear bomb. The main challenge for terrorist organizations seeking this capability is finding sufficient fissile material. Approximately 8 kilograms of plutonium or 25 kilograms of highly enriched uranium (HEU) is necessary for a bomb. Since 9/11, the United States, Russia, the IAEA, and other partners have taken on a number of efforts to decrease the risks of terrorists accessing nuclear material. United Nations (UN) Security Council Resolution 1540, the 2005 Amendment to the Convention on the Physical Protection of Nuclear Material, and the 2005 International Convention for the Suppression of Acts of Nuclear Terrorism all seek to increase global cooperation to prevent nuclear terrorism. Overall, the global stocks of HEU and plutonium are decreasing, but the sheer volume of global fissile material makes this an on-going challenge and the U.S. budget for these activities has recently been cut.

Unlike nuclear-armed states, it would be relatively difficult to deter terrorists from taking action.[96] In other words, if efforts to keep nuclear weapons out of terrorist hands fail even once, we may very well witness a nuclear 9/11.

Conclusion

This chapter examined the prospects for the next nuclear war. While we all hope that nuclear weapons will never be used again, this chapter suggests that as long as nuclear weapons and geopolitical conflict exist, there remains a nonzero risk of a nuclear exchange. To analyze this threat, this chapter looked to the only pre-

---

95. Mark Fitzpatrick, *Overcoming Pakistan's Nuclear Dangers* (Adelphi Series 443, London: International Institute for Strategic Studies, 2014).

96. For a strategy to deter terrorism, see Matthew Kroenig and Barry Pavel, "How to Deter Terrorism," *Washington Quarterly* 35, No. 2 (2012): 21-36.

vious instance of nuclear use, presented the theoretical mechanisms by which nuclear war might transpire, and identified the nuclear-armed actors and related conflicts that could result in nuclear war.

Fortunately, a next nuclear war is not preordained and there are a number of steps that the United States can take to reduce the risk. The first and most important step is to openly recognize, understand, and acknowledge the threat. U.S. leaders rarely talk about nuclear war. When authorities discuss the litany of threats posed by the spread of nuclear weapons, a frank discussion of nuclear war is often absent. For example, in explaining why he is opposed to allowing Iran to develop nuclear weapons, President Obama said:

> In addition to the profound threat that it poses to Israel, one of our strongest allies in the world; in addition to the outrageous language that has been directed toward Israel by the leaders of the Iranian government—if Iran gets a nuclear weapon, this would run completely contrary to my policies of nonproliferation. The risks of an Iranian nuclear weapon falling into the hands of terrorist organizations are profound. It is almost certain that other players in the region would feel it necessary to get their own nuclear weapons. So now you have the prospect of a nuclear arms race in the most volatile region in the world, one that is rife with unstable governments and sectarian tensions. And it would also provide Iran the additional capability to sponsor and protect its proxies in carrying out terrorist attacks, because they are less fearful of retaliation.[97]

President Obama never explicitly argued that a nuclear-armed Iran could result in a nuclear attack against the United States, Israel, or other states. Perhaps the threat was meant to be implicit in the

---

97. Jeffrey Goldberg, "Obama to Iran and Israel: 'As President of the United States, I Don't Bluff,'" *The Atlantic*, March 2, 2012.

discussion. Or perhaps Obama and others like him do not want to be accused of hysteria for trumpeting the alarm on such a low risk, high consequence outcome. Regardless of the cause of this reticence, nuclear war is a possible, and the most severe, consequence of nuclear weapons proliferation. U.S. leaders should explicitly confront this uncomfortable truth head on. After all, if we do not accurately articulate the threat, it will be difficult to adequately address it.

Elites in others states are less shy about broaching the subject. North Korean leaders regularly threaten nuclear use.[98] Pakistan's leaders have boasted to British officials about how quickly they could launch a nuclear attack against India.[99] Chinese state-owned media has proudly reported the death and destruction that a Chinese nuclear attack could inflict on the United States.[100] And President Putin recently explained to a youth group in Russia, "that Russia is one of the world's biggest nuclear powers. These are not just words–this is the reality. What's more, we are strengthening our nuclear deterrent capability."[101]

Once U.S. leaders more frankly acknowledge the threat of nuclear war, they must work with their counterparts abroad to take the necessary steps to stop it. This means taking a variety of steps to stabilize relations among existing nuclear powers. Most importantly, however, it means promoting strong nonproliferation policies to prevent the spread of nuclear weapons to more countries. With

---

98. For example, "North Korea ramps up nuclear rhetoric as UN vote looms," *BBC World News*, March 7, 2013, available from *www.bbc.com/news/world-asia-21698728*.

99. Nicholas Watt, "Pakistan boasted of nuclear strike on India within eight seconds," *The Guardian*, June 15, 2012.

100. Quoted in "China reveals its ability to nuke the US: Government boasts about new submarine fleet capable of launching warheads at cities across the nation," *Daily Mail*, November 2, 2013.

101. President of Russia, "Seliger 2014 National Youth Forum," August 29, 2014, full transcript available from *eng.kremlin.ru/transcripts/22864*.

each additional state that joins the nuclear club, the probability of the next nuclear war occurring in our lifetimes increases by some unknown margin. While the probabilities involved may be low, they might be just enough.

CHAPTER 6

After Armageddon: The Potential Political Consequences of Third Use

Matthew Fuhrmann

Nuclear weapons have thankfully not been used in war since 1945. The nonuse of the world's most destructive weapon for 70 years makes it tempting to conclude that nuclear weapons are relics of a bygone era. The possibility of another nuclear attack, according to this line of thinking, is remote. This view may be correct—and hopefully it is—but there is some cause for pessimism. Several alarming incidents during the Cold War brought the Soviet Union and the United States to the brink of nuclear war: Soviet leader Nikita Khrushchev threatened to unleash nuclear attacks if Western forces did not withdraw from West Berlin during crises in 1958-59 and 1961; an American U-2 spy plane accidently ventured into Soviet airspace during the height of the Cuban Missile Crisis in October 1962; the United States ordered DEFCON 3, thereby placing nuclear forces on alert, during the 1973 Yom Kippur War to deter Soviet involvement in the conflict; and a North Atlantic Treaty Organization (NATO) exercise, known as Able Archer 83, caused the Soviet Union to make preparations for nuclear war in 1983.

The world remains a dangerous place in the post-Cold War era. It does not take too much imagination to envision a scenario in which nuclear weapons could be used in today's environment. India and Pakistan threatened nuclear escalation during the 1999 Kargil War, and again following the 2001 Indian parliament attack. A future

Indo-Pakistani crisis could spiral out of control, leading to an accidental or intentional nuclear exchange. North Korea has made multiple nuclear threats since its first nuclear test in 2006. If backed into a corner, a desperate Kim Jung-un may carry out his threat to turn Seoul into a fireball. There have been three serious crises in the Taiwan Strait involving China and the United States—in 1954-55, 1958, and 1995. A fourth crisis, if it occurs, could escalate to a dangerous level.

Thinking about nuclear war scenarios is unpleasant. Indeed, it is depressing to imagine an event that could cause such widespread death and destruction. Studying this subject takes us into the "dark side" of international relations.[1] Uncomfortable as it may be, it is important to consider what might happen if nuclear weapons are used for a third time. How might nuclear use change the world in which we live?

Little scholarly literature in political science addresses this question. On one hand, it is easy to see why this is the case. Everyone understands that a nuclear attack has the potential to inflict catastrophic damage, possibly wiping entire countries off the map. Any additional political consequences seem trivial when compared to the human costs of nuclear war. Most scholarly thinking, therefore, has been devoted to the causes of war in the nuclear age. We seek to understand why wars occur and when nuclear deterrence might fail, in part, to offer guidance on how countries can further reduce the danger of armed conflict in the shadow of nuclear weapons.[2] This is perfectly reasonable, and I have framed some of my own

---

1. This phrase is borrowed from Robert Pape, who characterizes the study of military coercion as "the dark side of international relations." Robert Pape, *Bombing to Win: Air Power and Coercion in War* (Ithaca, NY: Cornell University Press, 1996), 3.

2. As Ronald Krebs writes, "the field's overriding concern was how to prevent a catastrophe in which millions would perish. This understandable focus on the causes of war came at the expense of research into its consequences." Ronald Krebs, "In the Shadow of War: The Effects of Conflict on Liberal Democracy," *International Organization* 63, No. 1 (Winter 2009): 177-210.

research along these lines.[3]

However, there is value in thinking through the possible political effects of the third use of nuclear weapons. First, this exercise can help us better understand a key puzzle in international relations: Why haven't nuclear weapons been used since 1945?[4] Part of the answer has to do with the human costs of a nuclear attack, but this cannot be the full story. A nuclear detonation in a large city could kill several hundred thousand civilians, but one can also imagine a nuclear use scenario in which few people die. One military advantage of nuclear bombs is that they can destroy "hardened" targets more effectively than conventional weapons. The United States, in theory, could launch a nuclear attack against a remote weapons of mass destruction (WMD) facility in the middle of a desert where there are few, if any, civilians for miles.[5] Such an attack may not kill any more people than a conventional strike would. Why have countries not used nuclear weapons in this type of scenario? We can more fully appreciate this issue by delving deeper into the political costs of nuclear attacks. As this chapter will show, the third use of nuclear weapons carries significant costs for the attacker, even if few people are killed as a result.

Second, from a policy standpoint, we risk underestimating the costs of nuclear use if we neglect the possible political consequences. Few credible analysts would suggest that a nuclear attack would

---

3. See, for example, Matthew Fuhrmann and Todd S. Sechser, "Signaling Alliance Commitments: Hand-Tying and Sunk Costs in Extended Nuclear Deterrence," *American Journal of Political Science* 58, No. 4 (October 2014): 919-935.

4 . Nina Tannenwald, *The Nuclear Taboo: The United States and the Non-Use of Nuclear Weapons Since 1945* (New York: Cambridge University Press, 2008); and T.V. Paul, *The Tradition of Nonuse of Nuclear Weapons* (Palo Alto, CA: Stanford University Press, 2009).

5. This is similar to a scenario discussed in Daryl Press, Scott Sagan, and Benjamin Valentino, "Atomic Aversion: Experimental Evidence on Taboos, Traditions, and the Non-Use of Nuclear Weapons," *American Political Science Review* 107, No. 1 (February 2013): 188-206.

not be costly. But significant costs may be "hidden," especially in cases where a country is not directly involved in nuclear use, either as the attacker or the target. The analysis that follows reveals that there are significant political risks associated with the third use of nuclear weapons. Once we take stock of these consequences, nuclear use seems even more cataclysmic than when we focus on the human costs alone.

This chapter considers the possible political ramifications of the bomb's third use. Lacking crystal balls, it is impossible to know for sure how world politics might change following a nuclear attack. Reaching definitive conclusions about something that has not happened is exceedingly difficult, and this inevitably requires a fair amount of speculation. This chapter does not intend to predict the future. It instead has three main goals: (1) to identify some of the conceivable political consequences of nuclear use; (2) to discuss variables that are likely to shape the degree to which these costs materialize; and (3) to comment on what my analysis teaches us about the role of nuclear weapons in world politics. The sections that follow address these issues in turn.

Potential Political Effects of the Third Use of Nuclear Weapons

This section considers some of the possible consequences of a nuclear attack. Before proceeding, some key points warrant further clarification. I focus on the political effects of nuclear use, largely leaving aside the numerous humanitarian, social, environmental, and economic consequences that would no doubt arise from a nuclear strike. Non-political issues associated with nuclear use are critically important, but they fall outside the scope of this particular chapter. Additionally, my analysis centers on the possible third use of nuclear weapons. The bomb's third use could lead to unrestrained nuclear warfare, but this chapter is not designed to assess the consequences of nuclear holocaust scenarios. Nuclear escalation is one conceivable consequence of a nuclear attack, and I discuss this possibility below, but I do not strive to comprehensively analyze the political consequences of total nuclear war.

The list of political costs that could arise from nuclear use is practically endless. I focus on some of the most significant consequences, grouping them into four main categories: (1) military escalation and the diffusion of armed conflict, (2) political blowback for the nuclear user, (3) damage to the nonproliferation regime, and (4) erosion of democracy. All of the consequences discussed below could plausibly result from a nuclear attack. This does not imply, however, that they would automatically materialize.

Military Escalation and the Diffusion of Armed Conflict

The third use of nuclear weapons could ignite an ongoing military conflict. Whether nuclear use leads to further military escalation depends, in part, on how the target state responds. If the target also possesses a nuclear arsenal, there would be significant pressure to launch a retaliatory nuclear strike. The third use of nuclear weapons, then, could quickly lead to the fourth use. After that, the conflict could escalate from limited to total nuclear war. Of course, even if the target has the capacity to strike back with its arsenal, nuclear retaliation is by no means guaranteed. The target may instead choose to launch a stiff conventional response, or surrender and not respond at all.[6] However, there is a non-trivial danger that using nuclear weapons could lead to unrestrained military escalation.

The level of escalation may depend on actors other than the nuclear user and the target. Nuclear use could pull other countries, especially powerful ones, into an ongoing war. During the Cold War, most of the plausible nuclear attack scenarios involved the

---

6. A target contemplating retaliation with nuclear weapons would have to weigh the benefits of attacking against the costs. A state might choose not to strike back with atomic weapons, for instance, if it believed that doing so would cause it to suffer further nuclear punishment, especially if the issue at stake was non-vital.

United States and the Soviet Union. The situation is different today: Many dangerous flashpoints in the world center on disputes
between regional powers, like India and Pakistan. When regional
powers armed with nuclear arsenals fight, there is often significant
pressure on other countries to intervene. During the 1999 Kargil
War, for example, the United States actively sought to prevent nuclear escalation. After U.S. intelligence detected the movement of
Pakistani nuclear weapons, President Bill Clinton warned Pakistani
leader Nawaz Sharif not to launch a nuclear attack, and this may
have helped bring an end to the conflict. If a regional nuclear power
followed through on an atomic threat, it would likely be difficult
for the United States to remain on the sidelines. Washington may
decide to intervene militarily, to deter further nuclear escalation.
The prospect of suffering military punishment at the hands of a
superpower may de-escalate a war, as it did in the case of Kargil.

Yet superpower intervention could further escalate tensions. Should
the United States join a limited nuclear war, the American arsenal
could be on the table. Pressure might mount, especially if there
were high casualties for U.S. forces, to launch retaliatory nuclear strikes against the initial nuclear user. Imagine, for the sake of
illustration, that North Korea launched a surprise nuclear attack
against Japan or South Korea. The United States may intervene
to defend its allies. If it did, Washington would surely prefer to
prevail using conventional military power only. However, if the
conflict persisted, some may come to believe that America could
not "win"—at least not at an unacceptable cost—by continuing to
fight at the conventional level. The end result, if this kind of thinking prevailed, could be an American nuclear response. Not only
does this stylized example illustrate how superpower intervention
could intensify an ongoing war, it also underscores that the third
use of nuclear weapons might lead to nuclear retaliation even if the
target is nonnuclear.

There are other, less obvious ways that a nuclear attack could lead
to the further spread of military conflict. Research shows that war

undermines public health.[7] Armed conflict can expose individuals to conditions that are conducive to the spread of disease, reduce the resources available for public health, and destroy critical infrastructure, like hospitals. One can imagine that the third use of nuclear weapons might create a severe public health crisis in the target country. Hundreds of thousands of civilians could be killed or injured, and medical help might not be readily available. The public health emergency that would likely ensue from a nuclear attack, combined with widespread panic in the civilian population, could undermine stability in the target country, potentially raising the risk of political violence or civil war.

The environmental consequences of a nuclear attack could also fuel instability in the target. A rich literature suggests that environmental degradation increases the risk of conflict, in part, by causing resource scarcity.[8] A nuclear attack would severely damage the surrounding environment, potentially rendering large portions of land uninhabitable. Moreover, food and water supplies could be contaminated. People may believe that it is unsafe to consume resources from the target, even if the food supply is unaffected by the nuclear blast, leading to further resource shortages. All of this could provoke a competition over scarce resources, potentially breeding conflict or civil war in the target country.

Chaos in the target state could have consequences for neighboring states, too. War is known to create refugee problems. As a result of the ongoing Syrian Civil War, for instance, more than 2 million civilians have fled Iraq, Lebanon, Jordan, Turkey, and elsewhere. Individuals may flee conflict zones because their homes are de-

---

7. See, for example, Hazem Adam Ghobarah, Paul Huth, and Bruce Russett, "Civil Wars Kill and Maim People—Long After the Shooting Stops," *American Political Science Review* 97, No. 2 (May 2003): 189-202; and Zaryab Iqbal, *War and the Health of Nations* (Palo Alto, CA: Stanford University Press, 2010).

8. Henrik Urdal, "People vs. Malthus: Population Pressure, Environmental Degradation, and Armed Conflict Revisited," *Journal of Peace Research* 42, No. 4 (July 2005): 417-434.

stroyed or due to concerns about their future safety. In any case, massive refugee flows can have significant political consequences. Most notably, the presence of refugees from neighboring states increases the likelihood that a country will experience political turmoil and armed conflict.[9] A nuclear attack could produce a similar sequence of events on a larger scale.

Civilians in the target country could flee to neighboring states in droves. Many would leave due to the belief that radioactive fallout from a nuclear blast makes it unsafe to remain in the country. Others may flee, even if they live far from the blast site, because they fear additional nuclear attacks. Neighboring countries would probably be ill-equipped to take on massive refugee flows. At the very least, this could create a major humanitarian crisis. Consider what happened following the March 2011 accident at Japan's Fukushima nuclear power plant. Widespread radioactive contamination forced many residents to flee the surrounding area. Two years after the disaster, there were still 83,000 nuclear refugees who were unable to return home.[10] The large-scale movement of people following a nuclear attack could raise the risk of conflict in neighboring countries by sapping public resources, inciting ethnic tensions, or spreading fear and uncertainty. Anticipating the problems associated with taking on refugees on a large scale, potential host countries might deny entry to civilians from the target country. If this happens, refugees themselves might turn to violence, in a desperate attempt to gain sanctuary in a neighboring state.

The third use of nuclear weapons could also have long-term consequences for international conflict. It is widely believed that conflict begets conflict.[11] In other words, once two countries fight, they are

9. Idean Salehyan and Kristian Skrede Gleditsch, "Refugees and the Spread of Civil War," *International Organization* 60, No. 2 (Spring 2006): 335-366.

10. Martin Fackler, "Japan's Nuclear Refugees, Still Stuck in Limbo," *New York Times*, October 1, 2013: available from *www.nytimes.com/2013/10/02/world/asia/japans-nuclear-refugees-still-stuck-in-limbo.html?_r=0.*

11. See, for example, Paul Diehl and Gary Goertz, W*ar and Peace in Interna-*

more likely to experience future military disputes. War, therefore, can lead to a vicious cycle that is difficult to reverse. It is no accident, according to this perspective, that countries such as India and Pakistan fight repeatedly over similar issues. Why do many conflicts recur? Part of the answer is that armed conflict creates grievances and leads to resentment and distrust, which increases the likelihood of future conflict. For example, there is still bad blood between Japan and South Korea over atrocities committed by Imperial Japan during World War II. Today, due to persistent feelings of resentment, the leaders of these two countries are reportedly "barely on speaking terms."[12] The use of nuclear weapons would likely result in widespread bitterness toward the nuclear user among individuals in the target country. As a result, once two countries fight a nuclear war, they are likely to fight again in the future. The consequences of nuclear use for international conflict, therefore, could persist long after fighting in the nuclear war stops. Nuclear use could severely exacerbate an existing interstate rivalry, or lead to the onset of a new one.

Political Blowback for the Nuclear User

The preceding discussion highlights some of the ways in which nuclear use could be damaging for international security. In this section, I focus on consequences that are unique to the nuclear user.[13] I highlighted the most direct such cost above: The user could suffer nuclear or conventional retaliation from the target or from third parties. Yet the possible costs for the attacker do not end there.

---

tional Rivalry (Ann Arbor, MI: University of Michigan Press, 2000).

12. Martin Fackler and Ghoe Sang-Hun, "A Growing Chill Between South Korea and Japan Creates Problems for the U.S.," *New York Times*, November 23, 2013, available from *www.nytimes.com/2013/11/24/world/asia/a-growing-chill-between-south-korea-and-japan-creates-problems-for-the-us.html*.

13. The discussion in this section draws partially on *Nuclear Weapons and Coercive Diplomacy* (Cambridge: Cambridge University Press, 2016).

A state that carried out the third use of nuclear weapons could experience other kinds political blowback.

A leader who carries out a nuclear attack could put his or her political future at risk. The third use of nuclear weapons would shatter a tradition of nuclear nonuse that has persisted for decades, a point that I will revisit in the subsequent section. Other countries are therefore likely to be threatened by the nuclear user's actions. They may seek to remove him or her from power through a foreign imposed regime change (FIRC). In the past, the United States has used FIRCs to punish leaders who pursued policies that were inimical to American interests. Washington covertly removed Mohammad Massaddegh from power in Iran during the 1950s and attempted to eliminate Cuban leader Fidel Castro on numerous occasions in the 1960s, to cite a couple of particularly infamous examples. The United States has also removed foreign leaders from power overtly, as in the case of Saddam Hussein during the 2003 Iraq War. It is not too hard to imagine that a leader who used nuclear weapons might suffer a similar fate. International actors may be unnecessary to remove the nuclear user from power. The use of nuclear weapons could incite domestic unrest, possibly triggering a domestic revolt that forces the nuclear user to step down.

Using nuclear weapons could complicate a state's relations with friendly nations. Countries often strain their alliance relationships when they take aggressive actions. For example, the United States was displeased when British and French troops invaded the Suez Canal zone in 1956. The Soviet Union was similarly alarmed when one of its protégés, North Korea, seized a U.S. military vessel known as the USS Pueblo in 1968. Alliances are particularly likely to become strained when there is the possibility of nuclear escalation. Many leaders in Western Europe were incensed by discussions of nuclear use in the United States during the Korean War (1953), the Indochina War (1954), and the Berlin crises (1958-59 and 1961). Soviet leader Nikita Khrushchev likewise became deeply concerned when Fidel Castro privately advocated for preventive nuclear strikes against the United States during the Cuban Mis-

sile Crisis. As a result of this episode, Khrushchev believed that
he could no longer trust Castro. When the crisis ended the Soviets
removed their tactical nuclear weapons from Cuba (the existence
of which the United States did not know at the time) that they initially intended to keep on the island. Castro's mercurial behavior
thus cost him weapons that could have been vital to his security.
The actual use of nuclear weapons could have profound effects on
alliance relationships. Allies may turn their backs on the nuclear
user or, at the very least, lose confidence in that state. The nuclear
user may be left with few, if any, friends.

In addition to causing a state to lose friends, using nuclear weapons may create enemies. Other states may align against the nuclear user, seeking to contain that state in the long-term. Countries
often form military alliances to counter common threats.[14] As the
old adage goes, an enemy of an enemy is a friend. Because other
countries are likely to find a state that uses nuclear weapons highly
threatening, they may unite against it by forging formal alliances.
By ganging up on the nuclear user in an attempt to contain it, the
international community would likely frustrate the user's ability to
pursue its interests in the realm of foreign policy. Imagine if China
used nuclear weapons in a future crisis with one of its regional rivals. That would likely change the way that many states perceive
Beijing's intentions, causing them to be more wary of China's rise
than they otherwise would be. Countries in Asia might therefore
actively contain China, to meet what they perceive as a growing
threat. In the end, China, a country whose grand strategy is based
partially on the notion of a "peaceful rise," may end up worse off
than it would have been in the absence of a nuclear attack.

The nuclear user could also become internationally isolated in other
ways. Countries might levy harsh economic sanctions against that
state or terminate commercial ties altogether. It is also conceivable
that states might sever diplomatic relations, leaving the nuclear

14. Stephen Walt, *The Origins of Alliances* (Ithaca, NY: Cornell University
Press, 1987).

user politically cut off from the rest of the world. Additionally, being labeled as a pariah could undermine a country's international influence.

Damage to the Nonproliferation Regime

The third use of nuclear weapons could undermine the nuclear nonproliferation regime. As noted above, there is a 70-year tradition of nuclear nonuse. Countries had opportunities to use nuclear weapons on a number of occasions, including some of those referenced above, but they refrained from doing so each time. In a few instances—notably the Vietnam War and the Soviet-Afghan War—nuclear powers accepted defeat before using their nuclear arsenals. The persistent absence of nuclear use has led to the creation of a "nuclear taboo."[15] This taboo brings stability to world politics by giving states greater confidence that they will not be subjected to unprovoked nuclear attacks. The third use of nuclear weapons, however, could shatter the nuclear taboo.

Using nuclear weapons for a third time might set a dangerous precedent—namely, that it is acceptable to use atomic bombs to resolve interstate disputes.[16] By changing the rules of the game, nuclear use could make future nuclear attacks more likely. To illustrate, consider how the use of nuclear weapons during the 1982 Falklands War might have affected the nuclear taboo. Britain carried nuclear weapons—specifically nuclear depths bombs—to the South Atlantic after Argentina occupied the disputed Falkland Islands. What if Britain had used one of those bombs, either intentionally or accidentally? Some may find this possibility farfetched, but if it had happened, it may have changed the way that countries

---

15. Tannenwald, *The Nuclear Taboo.*

16. Scott Sagan, "Realist Perspectives on Ethical Norms and Weapons of Mass Destruction," in Sohail Hashemi and Steven Lee, eds., *Ethics and Weapons of Mass Destruction: Religious and Secular Perspectives* (Cambridge: Cambridge University Press, 2004).

thought about nuclear weapons. Up until that point, the bomb had not been used in war for 37 years, contributing to the perception that "responsible" countries do not use such a destructive weapon. However, if Britain had broken the nuclear taboo, other nuclear powers might have believed that they too could use atomic weapons. Nuclear arsenals, then, may have come to play a bigger role in world politics. This brings me to a related point.

Nuclear use may foment nuclear proliferation. One effective non-proliferation strategy is to make the world think that nuclear weapons are utterly useless. If having a nuclear arsenal provides no benefits, why would anyone want to build one? The third use of nuclear weapons could cultivate the opposite perception—that possessing the bomb allows one to get their way in international relations. This was one unintended consequence of the nuclear attacks against Hiroshima and Nagasaki. At the time, most observers believed that using nuclear weapons helped the United States end the Pacific War on favorable terms.[17] This perception fueled widespread interest in nuclear weapons, particularly in the Soviet Union. If nuclear weapons are again seen as useful for coercing other states, interest in atomic arsenals could spike globally.

The preceding logic assumes that states desire nuclear weapons for offensive diplomatic purposes. Yet nuclear arsenals are useful primarily for defense.[18] Even status quo oriented countries, then, might seek nuclear weapons following their third use. Those states might do so to protect themselves from nuclear blackmail or nuclear attacks. History shows that countries sometimes launch nuclear weapons programs after they are faced with perceived nuclear threats. During the 1950s, for instance, the United States

---

17. Scholars continue to debate the role that the U.S. atomic bombings played in ending the Pacific War. See Tsuyoshi Hasegawa, *Racing the Enemy: Stalin, Truman, and the Surrender of Japan* (New York: Belknap Press, 2006); and Richard Frank (Downfall: The End of the Imperial Japanese Empire, New York: Penguin Books, 2001).

18. Sechser and Fuhrmann, *Nuclear Weapons and Coercive Diplomacy.*

brandished its nuclear arsenal in two crises with China in the Taiwan Strait. This caused officials in Beijing to believe that they were vulnerable to U.S. pressure in the absence of a nuclear deterrent. As the Chinese official statement issued after its first nuclear test in 1964 stated, China became a nuclear weapons state to "oppose the U.S. imperialist policy of nuclear blackmail and nuclear threats."[19] The third use of nuclear weapons could cultivate a sense of vulnerability in nonnuclear countries, similar to what China felt in the 1950s, causing them to seek a nuclear arsenal. It is not unreasonable to suppose that China's use of nuclear weapons in a future crisis with Taiwan, for example, might motivate some of the other countries with whom Beijing has ongoing disputes—Brunei Indonesia, Japan, Malaysia, the Philippines, Thailand, and Vietnam—to go nuclear.

There are, of course, significant costs associated with building nuclear weapons. In some cases, launching a bomb program may harm a state's security. As underscored by Israel's attacks against Iraq (1981) and Syria (2007), countries suspected of pursuing the bomb may be vulnerable to preventive military strikes. Some states might therefore hesitate to proliferate even if the third use of nuclear weapons leaves them feeling threatened. They may instead opt for another strategy: building the technical capacity to proliferate without actually building nuclear bombs. This strategy, known as "nuclear hedging," allows a state to quickly build a crude bomb in the event of a crisis. It is a potentially attractive path because it allows a country to have its cake (by being able to proliferate quickly if necessary) and eat it too (by skirting some of the costs associated with pursuing nuclear weapons). Some have argued that this is precisely the strategy that Iran is adopting today; Japan is another state believed to be engaging in nuclear hedging.[20] If states opt for this approach, the third use of nuclear weapons could lead to the diffu-

---

19. John Lewis and Xue Litai, *China Builds the Bomb* (Palo Alto, CA: Stanford University Press, 1991), 1.

20. Ariel Levite, "Never Say Never Again: Nuclear Reversal Revisited," *International Security* 27, No. 3 (Winter 2002-03): 59-88.

sion of advanced nuclear capabilities. Countries may not immediately weaponize those capabilities, but the presence of additional "latent nuclear powers" could undermine international security.[21]

Another use of nuclear weapons could weaken key international institutions, like the Nuclear Nonproliferation Treaty (NPT). The NPT allows five countries to possess nuclear weapons, and requires everyone else to give up the nuclear option. Many scholars and policymakers credit the treaty with restraining the further spread of nuclear weapons. In the early-1960s, President John F. Kennedy famously predicted that 15 or 20 countries could build nuclear weapons in the coming two decades. Yet after the NPT entered into force in 1970, only four states proliferated: India, North Korea, Pakistan, and South Africa. According to NPT advocates, many more countries would have proliferated if the treaty had not been created. Today, the NPT has near-universal membership: all but four countries are members.[22] However, the third use of nuclear weapons could cause states to withdraw from the treaty, which is within their right per Article X of the agreement, so long as they provide 90 days advanced notice. Countries who seek nuclear weapons, alternatively, could remain in the treaty and cheat on their NPT commitment. Either way, the glue that held the nonproliferation regime together for more than 40 years may no longer hold following the third use of nuclear weapons.

The discussion in this section so far assumes that the third use of nuclear weapons would negatively affect the nonproliferation regime. It is also possible, somewhat paradoxical, that nuclear use would result in a stronger regime. The international community often reacts to disasters by instituting sweeping reforms. Most of the major improvements to the nonproliferation regime since 1970 resulted from crises of confidence in existing measures. India's

---

21. Matthew Fuhrmann and Benjamin Tkach, "Almost Nuclear: Introducing the Nuclear Latency Dataset," *Conflict Management and Peace Science* 32, No. 4 (September 2015): 443-461.

22. The non-members are Israel, India, Pakistan, and North Korea.

nuclear test in 1974 led to the creation of the Nuclear Suppliers Group (NSG), a cartel designed to regulate trade in nuclear technology and materials. Iraq's violations of the NPT prior to the 1991 Persian Gulf War caused the international community to give the International Atomic Energy Agency (IAEA), the main enforcer of the NPT, more teeth through the 1997 Additional Protocol. And the international community sought to strengthen global export controls by passing United Nations (UN) Security Council Resolution 1540 after the public exposure of the A.Q. Khan network, a Pakistani-based operation that supplied nuclear weapon-related technology to Iran, Libya, and North Korea. As these examples illustrate, sweeping reforms are sometimes possible in a time of crisis. The third use of nuclear weapons would no doubt be horrific. It might therefore create a broad international consensus to strengthen nonproliferation norms, in an attempt to lower the odds that the bomb would be used a fourth time. This does not imply that the third use of nuclear weapons would be a good thing. The negative consequences would outweigh any marginal improvement in the nonproliferation regime resulting from nuclear use.

Erosion of Democracy

Political theorists and international lawyers have long recognized that war can undermine democratic governance—especially civil liberties. In time of war, leaders sometimes face pressures to degrade individual freedoms in the name of protecting state security. As one British lawyer put it, "it's always the case that the flame of civil liberties burns less brightly when surrounded by the smoke from bombed buses and tube trains."[23] President Abraham Lincoln, for example, famously suspended the writ of habeas corpus during the American Civil War, denying detainees the right to challenge unlawful imprisonment. Following the attack on Pearl Harbor, President Franklin Delano Roosevelt gave the military authority

---

23. Krebs, "In the Shadow of War," 184.

to remove Japanese-Americans from the west coast of the United States. And, more recently, civil liberties declined in the United States following the American response to the 9/11 attacks. Measures taken by Washington to prevent future terrorist attacks—such as the passage of the Patriot Act—had the consequence of reducing individual freedoms. As these examples underscore, war can put democratic values at risk in the short-term.

War may also have enduring, long-term effects on civil liberties, although this point is more widely contested in the academic literature. Measures that are put in place during times of emergency, according to one line of thinking, persist long after the fighting stops. Ronald Krebs aptly characterizes this view: "temporary states of emergency become permanent, emergency measures are incorporated into ordinary law, authorities employ emergency powers in everyday situations, and populations' civil liberties baselines adjust to new realities."[24] Others challenge this argument. Measures that are imposed during times of war, they argue, are lifted when peace returns.[25] Several historical cases support this view: The United States, for instance, reinstated habeas corpus once the civil war ended (although President Ulysses S. Grant temporarily suspended it again in some places during Reconstruction).

It is also possible that the long-term effects of war on democracy are positive. An executive's erosion of democracy during wartime could prompt a domestic backlash once fighting stops, leading to new measures that reign-in executive power. Some scholars point to the U.S. experience with the Vietnam War to substantiate this notion.[26] When the war ended, Congress passed the War Powers Resolution (1973), making it more difficult for the president to send U.S. forces abroad without congressional consent.

---

24. Ibid., 187-188.

25. Eric Posner and Adrian Vermeule, *The Executive Unbound: After the Madisonian Republic* (Oxford: Oxford University Press, 2011).

26. Krebs, 181-182

How might the third use of nuclear weapons influence democracy? There is general consensus that civil liberties are more likely to erode when states face intense threats.[27] A nuclear attack would likely trigger a sense of extreme panic in the target country. It is therefore possible that the target would face pressure to prioritize security above all else. When the conflict ended, the target might continue to impose restrictions on civil liberties, to forestall future nuclear attacks.

The bomb's third use might also erode democracy in states other than the target— particularly in those countries that could be vulnerable to nuclear strikes. Once the tradition of nuclear nonuse is broken, all states might change their views on the likelihood that they could suffer a nuclear attack. Given their obvious incentive to avoid atomic strikes, states may institute new measures to protect themselves from nuclear punishment. One possibility is that countries would give executives more sweeping powers, potentially at the risk of individual liberties, institutional checks and balances, and other hallmarks of democratic governance. Imagine if Russia launched a nuclear attack against Ukraine (leaving aside judgments about whether this is conceivable or not). Following such an attack, Russia's other rivals might come to believe that they are vulnerable to nuclear strikes. In addition, states that are enemies of nuclear powers other than Russia would probably face a heightened sense of insecurity. If Russia used nuclear weapons against Ukraine, for example, Japan and South Korea might fear that North Korea would be emboldened to follow suit against them. The potential victims of future nuclear attacks would naturally seek to enhance their security, and, in doing so, they may weaken their commitments to democracy.

Factors that Might Influence the Political Effects of Nuclear Use

We cannot know for certain, as noted previously, what would hap-

---

27. Ibid., 186.

pen if there is another nuclear attack. Some of the consequences identified above may emerge following the third use of nuclear weapons, but others may not. Whether costs materialize—and the degree to which they do so—will depend on a wide variety of considerations. This section focuses on some of the relevant factors. I identify the five "W's"—who, what, when, where, and why of nuclear third use—that could shape the nature and magnitude of the above political costs.

Factor #1: Who Uses Nuclear Weapons?

The characteristics of the nuclear user could play an important role. How powerful that state is, for example, may affect the price that it pays for using nuclear bombs. A superpower, like the United States today, may be relatively insulated from political blowback. Other states might be deterred from launching retaliatory strikes against the United States, for fear of provoking a broader conflict that they would likely lose. By contrast, potential punishers of the nuclear user may be less worried about military escalation if they are dealing with a non-superpower. The relative "rogueness" of the nuclear user would also be important. For a state that is largely cut off from the international community already—for example, North Korea—any additional isolation they might suffer as a result of using nuclear weapons could be trivial. Nuclear use, therefore, may be less costly for those states. Yet, for a country like China that is heavily integrated in the global economy, economic sanctions could have a devastating effect.

Some of the preceding discussion implies that the nuclear user would be a country. But this need not be the case. It is theoretically possible that the third user of nuclear weapons could be a terrorist group. Whether the user is a country or not would likely matter when it comes to the political fallout of a nuclear attack, a point on which I will elaborate later.

Factor #2: What is Targeted?

What the nuclear user destroys in an attack would also influence the political costs. Launching an attack against a city that kills 100,000 or more civilians is one thing. Using tactical bombs on the battlefield against an advancing army is another. Yet another is bombing a remote "hardened" target that results in relatively few casualties. The international community would likely deplore any use of nuclear weapons, but states would probably react the strongest to countervalue targeting. Thus, the political costs—especially the blowback for the nuclear user—would likely be greatest in cases where a state deliberately targets civilians.

Factor #3: When are Nuclear Weapons Used?

When a state launches a nuclear attack is another significant factor. It matters, in particular, whether nuclear use occurs during an ongoing war or in peacetime. Even conventional preventive attacks are controversial, as underscored by the 2003 Iraq War. A bolt from the blue nuclear attack would be a particularly strong violation of a longstanding international norm. Such an incident could draw extreme ire from other states, thus increasing the costs for the attacker. Things might be different if the third use of nuclear weapons occurred in the midst of a protracted conventional war. The political costs for the attacker, then, may be somewhat reduced in those cases, even if the blowback is still severe. Think, for the sake of illustration, about the U.S. attack on Hiroshima vis-à-vis a hypothetical preventive nuclear strike against Tokyo in 1940.

Factor #4: Where is the Bomb Used?

Against whom an attacker uses nuclear weapons could influence the consequences of nuclear use for world politics. Whether the target possesses nuclear weapons is one critical consideration. If the target is nonnuclear, the potential for nuclear escalation declines. At the same time, some of the non-military costs for the attacker could increase. Using the bomb against a nonnuclear state could be seen as particularly reprehensible,[28] and might trigger a stiffer response from the international community. If the target also possesses the bomb, there is a higher probability of nuclear retaliation. Those scenarios, then, are potentially more dangerous for international security. Yet the non-military costs might decline slightly, as others are less likely to perceive the attack as an attempt to bully a defenseless country.

The target's ability to cope with a nuclear attack might also be significant. Several of the political costs discussed previously may be worse when the target is unstable. In particular, countries that are already prone to political violence would probably be more prone to civil war following a nuclear attack. On top of this, unstable countries, which are also likely to be underdeveloped, may be relatively helpless when it comes to addressing the fallout from a nuclear attack. Life in a developed country would almost certainly be chaotic after a nuclear strike, too. But a state with the capacity to at least partially deal with an emergency might be able to lessen refugee problems and other environmental issues, although these problems would still be acute. Therefore, conflict might be more likely to diffuse when the target is weak (for example, Pakistan) than when it is strong (for example, the United States).

Factor #5: Why are Nuclear Weapons Used?

The reason a state used nuclear weapons represents a fifth key consideration. The third use of nuclear weapons could be deliberate or accidental. Indeed, many plausible nuclear attack scenarios during the Cold War and today involve non-authorized nuclear use. It was possible that during the Cuban Missile Crisis, for instance, a lo-

---

28. Paul Huth and Bruce Russett, "Deterrence Failure and Crisis Escalation," *International Studies Quarterly* 32, No. 1 (February 1988): 35.

cal Soviet commander in Cuba could have fired a nuclear weapon without explicit authorization from Moscow. If the third use of nuclear weapons occurs due to the actions of a rogue military officer, the nature of the political costs could change dramatically. For example, international attention might be focused on how to better secure existing nuclear arsenals, rather than on how to punish the nuclear user. This does not imply, of course, that a nuclear user would be absolved of any and all responsibility simply because an attack was accidental.

When attacks are deliberate, the intentions of the attacker also matter. First, it makes a difference whether others perceive its aims as offensive or defensive. Most deliberate uses of nuclear weapons that one can imagine serve a coercive purpose: The attacker hopes to change the behavior of the target by inflicting massive amounts of punishment, or impose its will militarily. However, not all coercive uses of nuclear weapons are the same. In some cases, the attacker seeks a return to the status quo ante. Using nuclear weapons to restore stability to a system that was challenged by a revisionist power may be viewed as more acceptable than launching a nuclear attack entirely for offensive purposes. Consider the 1991 Persian Gulf War. The United States tried to force Saddam Hussein from Kuwait, first with diplomacy and then with military force. Yet the international community did not view Washington as the aggressor. Most observers recognized that the United States was responding to Saddam's unprovoked invasion and occupation of a largely defenseless neighbor. In this type of case, nuclear use may be less costly than when the attacker's aims are perceived as offensive, as in the 2003 invasion of Iraq (note that there is some overlap here with factor #3).

Second, the attacker's specific goals are also relevant. Other countries would probably respond differently to the third use of nuclear weapons based on the stakes for the attacker. If the attacker is fighting for its survival, and especially if it was attacked first, others might understand why it resorted to the nuclear option, potentially lessening their willingness to retaliate diplomatically, politically,

or economically. By contrast, others may have a hard time empa-
thizing with a state that used nuclear weapons in pursuit of an important but non-vital objective, like forcing the target to hand over
disputed territory.

Conclusion: The Role of Nuclear Weapons in World Politics

Two points about the consequences of nuclear use are worth un-
derscoring. First, many of the political effects discussed in this
chapter—for example, the possibility of conflict escalation—are
straightforward, but others are less obvious. The effects of nuclear
use for democracy and civil war, in particular, have received relatively little attention in the literature. These things might seem
trivial when compared to the loss of hundreds of thousands of civilians. At the same time, we risk underestimating the effects of
nuclear use by neglecting the political costs of an atomic attack.
This chapter represents a modest attempt to discuss some of the
main political consequences; there are no doubt others that I have
not identified.

Second, there is important variation in the political costs of nuclear
use. All uses of atomic bombs are not created equal, even if they
produce similar human costs. Both a Pakistani tactical nuclear attack against advancing Indian conventional forces in a future war
and a North Korean nuclear attack on Seoul launched in response
to a mistaken false warning of an incoming American missile attack, for example, would produce horrific consequences, but they
would likely affect world politics in different ways. The "five W's"
of nuclear use discussed in this chapter offer a framework for understanding how the political costs might vary.

More generally, the analysis in this chapter speaks to the tradition of
nuclear nonuse.[29] Everyone understands that a nuclear attack would

29. Tannenwald, *The Nuclear Taboo*; and Paul, *The Tradition of Nonuse of Nuclear Weapons*.

be devastating for the target. However, my analysis reaffirms that the third use of nuclear weapons would also be quite costly for the attacker. A state that launched a nuclear attack would probably suffer enormous political blowback, and would do great damage to the nonproliferation regime (which is damaging to the extent that the attacker cares about limiting the spread of nuclear weapons). These costs help explain why countries have refrained from using nuclear weapons in war since 1945, although moral considerations also play an important role.

In addition, this chapter has implications for the benefits that states derive (and do not gain) from possessing a nuclear arsenal. Some have argued that atomic arsenals are useful tools of coercion and intimidation.[30] Nuclear weapons, according to this line of thinking, have benefits that extend well beyond deterrence. States can extract concessions more effectively or impose their will on others simply by raising the possibility of a nuclear attack. Others have challenged this view, arguing that nuclear weapons have little utility beyond deterring military conflict.[31] The reason is simple: It is difficult to make nuclear threats credible when the potential attacker's aims are compellent in nature (as opposed to deterrent). Recognizing that there is variation in the costs of nuclear use for the challenger helps us understand why nuclear weapons may be useful for some political purposes and not others. Consider a hypothetical scenario where China decides to attack Japan's third largest city, Osaka, after escalating conventional engagements over the Senkaku Islands. The costs for the attacker are greatest in this case because nuclear use occurred for offensive purposes during a crisis in which the attacker's national survival was not at stake. This is partially why this scenario is quite unlikely to occur. China is un-

---

30. See, for example, Pape, *Bombing to Win*; Kyle Beardsley and Victor Asal, "Winning with the Bomb," *Journal of Conflict Resolution* 53, No. 2 (March 2009): 278-301; and Matthew Kroenig, "Nuclear Superiority and the Balance of Resolve," *International Organization* 67, No. 1 (January 2013): 141-171.

31. Sechser and Fuhrmann, "Crisis Bargaining and Nuclear Blackmail," *International Organization* 67, No. 1 (2013): 173-195.

likely to carry out a strike that harms its strategic interests to such a degree. Japan and the United States would recognize this at the outset, and they are likely to dismiss Beijing's coercive nuclear threat as incredible. China thus will have a hard time wresting away the Senkakus from Japan by practicing nuclear coercion. In cases like this, then, states are unlikely to derive much political utility from their nuclear arsenals. By contrast, in deterrence, the costs of nuclear use for the challenger are smaller, and the stakes may be higher. A state's threat to launch a nuclear attack if it is invaded, therefore, may be deemed credible. Again, nuclear weapons may deter but they generally do not compel.[32]

Given the possible political costs of nuclear use detailed above, states would do well to take further measures to avoid the possibility of third use.

---

32. Ibid., 175.

ABOUT THE CONTRIBUTORS

W. SETH CARUS is a Distinguished Research Fellow at the Center for the Study of Weapons of Mass Destruction at the National Defense University. His research focuses primarily on issues related to biological warfare, including threat assessment, biodefense, and the history of biological warfare. He is co-author of *The Future of Weapons of Mass Destruction: Their Nature and Role in 2030* (2014) and author of *Defining "Weapons of Mass Destruction," Revised and Updated* (2012), both published by the National Defense University Press. Dr. Carus has been at NDU since 1997. He has a Ph.D. in International Relations from the Johns Hopkins University in Baltimore, Maryland.

MATTHEW FUHRMANN is an associate professor of political science at Texas A&M University. He is a former Stanton Nuclear Security Fellow at the Council on Foreign Relations and research fellow at the Belfer Center for Science and International Affairs at Harvard University. Dr. Fuhrmann is the author of *Atomic Assistance: How "Atoms for Peace" Programs Cause Nuclear Insecurity*, the co-author of *Nuclear Weapons and Coercive Diplomacy*, and the co-editor of *The Nuclear Renaissance and International Security*. His research has been published in a number of journals, including *American Journal of Political Science, British Journal of Political Science, International Organization, International Security, Journal of Conflict Resolution, Journal of Peace Research*, and *Journal of Politics*, among others. He has published opinion pieces in outlets such as the *Christian Science Monitor, Slate*, and *USA Today*.

REBECCA DAVIS GIBBONS is a Visiting Assistant Professor at Bowdoin College. Her current book project examines how the United States has employed various tools of hegemony to bring about participation in the nuclear nonproliferation regime. In 2013-2014, Dr. Gibbons held a Stanton Nuclear Security Fellowship at the RAND Corporation. She received a Ph.D. in government from Georgetown University, an M.A. in international security studies from Georgetown University, and a B.A. in psychological & brain sciences from Dartmouth College.

VICTOR GILINSKY is an independent consultant primarily on matters related to nuclear energy. He was a two-term commissioner of the U.S. Nuclear Regulatory Commission from 1975-1984, and before that Head of the Rand Corporation Physical Sciences Department. He holds a Bachelors of Engineering Physics degree from Cornell University and a Ph.D. in Physics from the California Institute of Technology, which gave him its Distinguished Alumni Award. He is a member of the American Physical Society and the Institute of Electrical and Electronics Engineers.

MATTHEW KROENIG is an associate professor of government and foreign service and a nonresident senior fellow at the Brent Scowcroft Center on International Security at the Atlantic Council. From July 2010 to July 2011, he was a Special Advisor in the Office of the Secretary of Defense on a Council on Foreign Relations International Affairs Fellowship; and he worked as a strategist in the Office of the Secretary of Defense in 2005. Dr. Kroenig has held fellowships from the Council on Foreign Relations, the National Science Foundation, the Belfer Center for Science and International Affairs at Harvard University, the Center for International Security and Cooperation at Stanford University, and the Institute on Global Conflict and Cooperation at the University of California. He is a life member of the Council on Foreign Relations.

JOHN MUELLER is Woody Hayes Senior Research Scientist at the Mershon Center as well as Adjunct Professor of political science at Ohio State University. He is also a Senior Fellow at the Cato Institute in Washington, DC. Among his books are *Chasing Ghosts: The Policing of Terrorism and Terror*, *Security and Money* (both with Mark Stewart), as well as *War, Presidents and Public Opinion*; *Astaire Dancing*; *Retreat from Doomsday: The Obsolescence of Major War*; *Quiet Cataclysm*; *Overblown*; *Atomic Obsession: Nuclear Alarmism from Hiroshima to Al-Qaeda*; *War and Ideas*; *Terrorism Since 9/11: The American Cases* (editor); and *A Dangerous World?* (co-editor). He is a member of the American Academy of Arts and Sciences, has been a John Simon Guggenheim Fellow, has received several teaching prizes, and in 2009 received the International Studies Association's Susan Strange Award that "recognizes a person whose singular intellect, assertiveness, and insight most challenge conventional wisdom and intellectual and organizational complacency in the international studies community."

HARVEY M. SAPOLSKY is Professor of Public Policy and Organization, Emeritus, at the Massachusetts Institute of Technology and the former Director of the MIT Security Studies Program. He has written extensively on U.S. and comparative science, defense, health and communication policies. In defense he has specialized in weapon acquisition policy, the defense industry, defense politics, national strategy, and military innovation. Professor Sapolsky has been a visiting professor at the University of Michigan and the U.S. Military Academy and a consultant to many government agencies, national commissions, and firms. His most recent books are *U.S. Defense Politics: the Origins of Security Policy* (with E. Gholz and C. Talmadge) and *U.S. Military Innovation Since the End of the Cold War: Creation Without Destruction* (edited with B. Friedman and B. Green).

HENRY SOKOLSKI is the Executive Director of the Nonprolif-eration Policy Education Center (NPEC). He previously served as Deputy for Nonproliferation Policy in the Department of Defense, and has worked in the Office of the Secretary of Defense's Office of Net Assessment, as a consultant to the National Intelligence Council, and as a member of the Central Intelligence Agency's Se-nior Advisory Group. In the U.S. Senate, Mr. Sokolski served as a special assistant on nuclear energy matters to Senator Gordon Humphrey (R-NH) and as a legislative military aide to Dan Quayle (R-IN). He was appointed by Congress to serve on both the Com-mission on the Prevention of Weapons of Mass Destruction Prolif-eration and Terrorism in 2008 and the Deutch WMD Proliferation Commission in 1999. Mr. Sokolski has authored and edited a num-ber of works on proliferation, including *Underestimated: Our Not So Peaceful Nuclear Future* (Strategic Studies Institute, 2016) and *Best of Intentions: America's Campaign Against Strategic Weapons Proliferation* (Praeger, 2001).